BRAND LOVE IS NOT ENOUGH

How would you feel about a bank that handled all of your financial needs efficiently, but made you feel like a dummy? In a relationship between two people, what the other person thinks of you (or what you believe they think of you) exerts great influence on the quality of your relationship. The same is true for your relationship with brands.

In this trailblazing book, Blackston extends his theory on consumer brand relationships introduced in the 1990s. He introduces a new construct called "brand's attitude," which complements the idea of brand image and introduces a typology of consumer relationships that is richer and more varied than the familiar concept of brand love. This construct describes more fully the two-way street that exists between consumers and brands, and fills a crucial gap in traditional branding literature in explaining consumers' brand purchasing and usage behavior.

Drawing on numerous actual examples and cases from a variety of different industries, and supported by 30 years of consumer data, *Brand Love is not Enough* should be on the shelf of any serious marketer or student of branding.

Max Blackston is a founding partner at BlackBar Consulting, USA. He is a brand strategist, market researcher, and consumer psychologist with a long track record of innovation in the consumer sciences. His work, in which he conceptualized the first original theory of consumer brand relationships, has gained wide recognition both in the academic world and by fellow practitioners, and has been published and reprinted in many countries.

BRAND LOVE IS NOT ENOUGH

A Theory of Consumer Brand
Relationships in Practice

Max Blackston

Routledge
Taylor & Francis Group

NEW YORK AND LONDON

First published 2018
by Routledge
711 Third Avenue, New York, NY 10017

and by Routledge
2 Park Square, Milton Park, Abingdon, Oxon, OX14 4RN

Routledge is an imprint of the Taylor & Francis Group, an informa business

Library of Congress Cataloging in Publication Data
A catalog record for this book has been requested

ISBN: 978-1-138-03981-0 (hbk)
ISBN: 978-1-138-03982-7 (pbk)
ISBN: 978-1-315-17562-1 (ebk)

Typeset in Bembo Std
by Swales & Willis Ltd, Exeter, Devon, UK

To Barbara

My muse and my unfailing support

CONTENTS

FIGURES

TABLES

PREFACE

The coming of age of brands coincided more or less with the start of my professional life in the 1960s. Brands had, of course, existed for a long time before then, but the status they now enjoy as major corporate assets had only then begun to be realized. Over the last nearly 50 years, hardly a day has passed that I have not discussed some aspect of brands or branding and, over this period, the vocabulary of branding has become ever wider and richer – from brand image and brand personality to brand equity. A brand is never "just" a brand; it is a brand leader, a mega brand, a niche brand, a power brand, an umbrella brand, and sometimes a ghetto brand. Brand management has embraced brand positioning, graduated to brand stewardship and brand engineering, and recently discovered brand love. Where do brand relationships fit into the brand conversation?

Brand Relationships – or Consumer Brand Relationships (CBR) – has replaced Brand Equity as the preferred term at the high ground of branding practice. Unheard of 30 years ago, when – to my knowledge – I was the first to use the term in print, it is now used to describe virtually any brand-consumer construct or interaction. The term has become so ubiquitous that it now verges on losing any specific meaning.

The current popularity of the term Consumer Brand Relationships is perhaps an explicit acknowledgment of the consumer as an active player in the creation of brands. Although that has always been the case, the internet and social media have ushered in an age of communicational democracy that potentially gives a voice to every consumer. Brand owners' narratives about their brands no longer dominate the space; brand advocacy – or its opposite – by individual consumers is now as important as mass communications. The expansion of digital forces and social media do certainly provide a new and powerful substrate for the expression and articulation of the relationships between brand and consumer; but the internet did not give rise to them. Consumer brand relationships are created in the consumer's mind, not in any other medium.

By default, most users of the term Brand Relationships – in a specific sense, as opposed to its use as a generic surrogate for the term Brand Equity – have in mind something analogous to interpersonal relationships (IPR). This is, of course, an "easy option," as it has permitted the wholesale adoption of an existing model and literature, in place of the development of grounded theories specific to consumer brand relationships. I believe that the IPR model is the wrong one – not because it is an easy option, but because it is wrong. Nothing better illustrates this than the focus on "Brand Love" as the nucleus of consumers' relationships with brands, around which orbit all its various satellite IPR constructs – dating, passion, fidelity, divorce, etc. Brand Love not only under-represents the variety and diversity of consumers' relationships with brands, but the construct itself is misconceived; unlike the love between people, brand love – or any other relationship between the brand and the consumer – exists totally inside the head of the consumer. It is manifest in a psychic space – not a social one – which means that brand love should be conceptualized as a psychological phenomenon, not as a sociological one.

This book describes and illustrates a psychological model of consumer brand relationships that originated in the theory and practice of Relational Psychology. It introduces a new construct, which I call brands' attitudes – what (the consumer believes that) the brand thinks; I demonstrate – both theoretically and via multiple case histories – how this construct complements the familiar construct of brand image (what the consumer thinks about the brand), and how it is the dialogue between the two – between consumers' image of a brand and consumers' projection of its attitudes – that determines the consumer brand relationship. The fact that both perspectives on the relationship with a brand reside in the mind of the consumer does not mean that we can afford either to ignore one of them, or confound the two. The Brand Love construct, as it is generally conceptualized, does just that; it is all about how the consumer loves the brand, and completely ignores the brand's response to the consumer's love. One-way, or unrequited, love is generally a most unsatisfactory type of relationship; unless the brand – the object of the consumer's feelings – in some way "returns" that love, then the consumer brand relationship remains unconsummated. While interpersonal love may superficially be a reasonable analogue of consumers' love for the brand, it provides no sustenance at all for describing the other side of the relationship.

The dialogue with the brand in the consumer's mind goes on whether or not there is anyone listening into it. Brand-consumer relationships exist independently of whether there is a feedback or response mechanism, which communicates something from the consumer to the brand's managers; they are inherent in the nature of what a brand means to consumers and in the nature of how relationships – of any sort – are formed. My aim is to describe these relationships, and to explain how they are created – with or without the intervention of a brand's managers – and how understanding, molding, and using these relationships should be an essential element in brand management.

My intention with this book is to provide a rigorous grounded theory of Consumer Brand Relationships, together with the fruit of more than 25 years of practical application of the theory. The broader aim is to encourage marketing professionals to move away from the brand monologue model of discourse with the consumer to one of dialogue, and to provide them with tools and constructs to help them do so.

In Chapter 1, I start by asking why, in many market research studies, even comprehensive measurements of consumers' perceptions of brands' images fail to provide a complete explanation of consumer behavior. I argue that brand image by itself is only one aspect of consumers' perceptions that influence behavior; there is a second and distinct aspect of consumers' perceptions, which I have termed "brands' attitudes," which are inferences made by the consumer about how the brand perceives him or her, and about how brands' behaviors create personal experiences for the consumer. The concept of brands' attitudes is introduced and illustrated via a series of brief case-studies and examples. Brand love is critically analyzed, and shown to be only one element of one of a number of possible consumer brand relationships.

Chapter 2 presents a theory of brands' relationships with consumers; as consumer brand relationships are totally a function of consumers' perceptions, I believe that a psychological theory is a more appropriate basis for the development of a consumer brand relationships model than a sociological one such as interpersonal relationships. Relational Psychology provides a very suitable model; one of its core concepts is object usage, in which inanimate relationship partners – so-called "Transitional Objects" – may be invested with the same type of characteristics – personality, motivations, attitudes, etc. – as animate ones. These concepts can be readily applied to the consumer brand relationship, inasmuch as a brand can legitimately be considered as a transitional object. The methodology for identifying consumers' relationships with a brand is an inferential one, based on the observation of the attitudes and behaviors of the consumer toward the brand, and the attitudes and behavior of the brand as perceived by the consumer. Consumer brand relationships result from the interaction of these two independent sets of perceptions; based on this definition, I introduce the Brand Relationship Map, a two-dimensional representation of brand relationships.

Chapters 3 through 6 deal with the many brand relationships I have analyzed – either from a distance using only the information that any interested party could acquire or from a closer perspective, with the benefit of a more informed knowledge base. Brand relationships can be mapped, using appropriate consumer research techniques, and many of the case histories are illustrated with the findings of research. Although a brand relationship is the result of a process between specific groups of consumers and a specific brand, it does not exist in a vacuum; the nature and history of the product category can both constrain and catalyze the formation of particular types of brand relationship. It is therefore instructive to examine relationships within the context of product categories, or types of product category, and this provides the structure for the following chapters that deal with brand relationships in practice.

Products that are used in or on the body – and extensions of the body, like clothes and houses – have a particular significance for all consumers. This is why relationships with brands in these categories – Food, Toiletries/Health and Beauty Aids, and Detergents and Laundry – share certain common characteristics. These products represent the classic packaged consumer goods categories, in which brands interact with and are evaluated by consumers almost on a daily basis. Using one of these brands means more than "solving" a functional problem; it also usually involves experiencing a range of associative memories, emotions, and fantasies – hedonic consumption. Brands' attitudes are the vehicle for transmitting the hedonic values of the brand. Chapter 3 contains in-depth case histories from each of these categories, and draws some generalized conclusions based on these cases.

The topic of Chapter 4 is prestige and luxury brands. Most brands satisfy a need – emotional or symbolic – over and above the strictly functional; because consumers' self-image and self-esteem are often so intimately bound up with – and even dependent on – prestige or luxury brands, relationships with them can be very strong – in both positive and negative senses – and completely override any functional considerations. Consumers' relationships with brands that serve as badges or as status symbols are therefore distinctive both in their nature and in their intensity. Case histories involving credit card brands and designer brands illustrate the delicate balance – between being prestigious and being unapproachable – that these brands have to achieve in their relationships with consumers.

The issue of risk – or perceived risk – is the subject of Chapter 5. In financial services like investment banking or insurance, or any category where there is a degree of objective risk for the consumer, the most appropriate types of brand can vary diametrically depending on how the consumer tolerates risk. Knowing the consumer's level of tolerance for risk is therefore essential in order to craft the most appropriate relationship with a financial brand. As a consequence, "one-stop-shopping" financial brands may find it hard to develop brand relationships suitable for all types of customer across the range of their services. Aside from financial services, there are a number of categories – for example, Over the Counter medications, or those involving new technology – where the consumer cannot easily evaluate the performance of the product, and where a level of implicit dependence on the brand may be necessary in order to reduce the level of perceived risk. Dependence can be a very strong brand relationship, which requires the brand to be seen as authoritative; authority, however, has to stay relevant, and brands once seen as authorities risk, because of complacent and/or presumptuous brands' attitudes, becoming merely has-beens.

Although corporate brands crop up in a number of chapters, Chapter 6 is focused exclusively on them, because the nature of a corporate brand is fundamentally different from that of a single-product brand. Consumers buy and use the products of multi-product corporate brands – like automobiles, computers, and telecommunications products – but their brand relationships are mostly determined by the corporate entity. All products which bear the corporate brand name share – to a greater or lesser extent – in the vicissitudes of the parent brand's relationships with its consumers; this is the first major difference. Second, like altering the direction of an oil tanker, changing the relationships of a corporate brand requires a much greater lead-time and resources, and usually involves a much higher risk. Two brand relationships – Trust and Customer Satisfaction – are key to successful corporate branding; Trust results from perceptions of the corporate brand's reliability and belief in its knowledge of its customers; Customer Satisfaction is based on being seen as pro-active *in the service of the customer*. These two Brand Relationships are mapped for corporate brands in several categories. The phenomenon of an individual product brand transcending its corporate parent has both advantages – for the individual product brand – and risks – for the corporate brand. Examples of both are discussed in the chapter.

Chapter 7 broadens the focus from specific categories of product or service, to describe a set of Universal Consumer Brand Relationships that are applicable in all product categories. These universals are broader "envelopes" into each of which a number of more specific brand relationships could be classified. There is a trade-off, because generalization inevitably entails a loss of precision and focus, so that universal brand relationships may not be as useful as category-specific ones for examining the relationships of brands in a specific category. However, in all product categories there are a set of common processes involved in brand-building; bringing new users into a brand's franchise and keeping them there, encouraging brand preference and loyalty, supporting a higher price and bigger margins, making more profit and – ultimately – building a branded business that financial markets value highly. Each of these processes is mediated by consumer brand relationships, and the set of Universal Brand Relationships is the necessary tool for obtaining a generalizable picture of the connections and pathways between the relational brand and a successful branded business.

Chapter 8 describes a formal statistical model, which measures the influence of each of the universal brand relationships on the size and strength of brand franchises, and ultimately on the value of branded businesses, as reflected in their stock market valuations. This model provides a link between the micro-level activities of consumer brand relationship management and macro-level market phenomena, and a guide for evaluating brand strategies designed to maximize the shareholder value of branded businesses. The chapter – and the book – concludes with a discussion about possible and probable future developments in consumers' relationships with brands.

In most categories in which the experienced brand analyst has more than a passing acquaintance with the structure of the market, the history of the brands and their current positioning, it is possible to develop a rough-textured map of the major brands' relationships. However, in order to refine this picture, or to explore relationships with different target groups, consumer research is necessary and can be very revealing. There is only one methodological message that I would like all readers to take out from this book, which is that the ubiquitous "focus" group discussion is not a suitable approach for exploring relationships between individual consumers and brands. This aside, I have preferred to put research in the appendix, because it deals with a number of methodological and technical issues, which will be of most interest to research practitioners and users. The methods – both qualitative and quantitative – used to research brands' relationships are essentially a specialized subset of the more general methodologies of consumer research. As such, they sub-serve the relationships concept, so the reader who is less interested in "how to do it" than in the ideas themselves can happily omit the appendix.

Some of the ideas in this book have already reached the public domain – either in journals or in the proceedings of conventions and seminars – and the many reactions to them from other marketing professionals as well as post-graduate students of marketing encourage me to believe that publishing them in book form will enrich the brand literature available for those both working in or studying the marketing disciplines.

ACKNOWLEDGMENTS

I am indebted to the many fellow practitioners, too numerous to mention, who over the years have enriched my understanding of brands and the practice of branding. Of all of these, I must single out two people – without one of them I would probably not have begun this journey, and without the other I would certainly not have got this far; they are, respectively, Dott. Luciano Poli of Milan, Italy, and Ed Lebar, my good friend and business partner. I must also thank Theodore Blackston for applying his graphical skills to make the many figures I have used more readily understandable.

1

THE I-MAGE GAP

The basic question I am addressing in this book is: What makes a brand successful? Why do people buy a specific brand, rather than one of its competitors' – or why do they buy that brand more often than the others? Let's ask the question in a very specific way: What is it that gets people lining up for hours to part with not inconsiderable sums of money the day after the latest i-thing goes on sale? Aside from the unique product design features and performance, the wealth of available apps, music and other content, the ineffable Apple/Jobs appeal, and memorable Super Bowl ads, what else is it that they are buying?

There are obviously several answers to this question – or rather several types of answers; many of them concern the physical nature of the brand – the attributes of the product or service itself – or the classic marketing variables – price, packaging, distribution, advertising, net presence. These are usually the easy questions to answer. The harder-to-answer questions concern what is sometimes referred to as the "essence" of the brand itself – the essential "i-ness" of an i-thing; not its physical characteristics, not how it performs or delivers – but the i-ntangibles of the brand.

Traditionally, the intangibles have gone under various headings – brand image, brand personality, brand associations, etc. Nowadays, many people would add another heading – which we might term "viralness" – to summarize the presence and proactivity of the brand on the internet. For the moment we will group all these brand-related concepts under the convenient and familiar heading of "brand image." At its very simplest, this may just consist of the answer to the question "do you like this brand?" Clearly this begs the question of why a consumer might like or dislike a brand, but none the less it ought to be a good starting point; if you are a brand manager, having people like your brand ought to be a good thing; the more consumers there are that like it, the more there will be that buy it; and the more that they like it, the more they should buy it – more frequently, more loyally. If only it was that simple; the problem is that this is – at best – only partially true. While people generally do not buy brands they don't like, the opposite is not necessarily true; many people like brands they do not buy – and sometimes they like them a lot.

In two recent studies conducted by my consulting firm – one in the USA and one in Mexico, together covering 128 brands in 20 different product categories – on average *about one in four of the people who never use a brand say they "love it" or "like it a lot."* Liking or loving a brand may be a necessary condition for buying it, but it is not sufficient.

Even if we say that reducing brand image to the single dimension of liking or even loving the brand is an over-simplification, and that we have to consider a broader range of consumers' perceptions of the brand, that does not solve the problem. Adding more of the same does not help; the same discontinuities between brand image and purchasing behavior can be found even when the former is measured in terms of a sophisticated and comprehensive array of brand image attributes and brand personality dimensions. A "strong" brand image – as we currently conceive it – may be a necessary condition for purchasing, but – by itself – it is insufficient to explain the kind of attachment to a brand that leads to purchasing – let alone the more committed behavior of repeated purchasing and brand loyalty. So is this the end of the story? Are we banging our heads up against the limitations of consumer science? Given that I ask such a question at the beginning of Chapter 1 of this book, the reader will rightly conclude that I do not believe so. Over the years that I have worked in marketing communications and consumer research, I have come to the conclusion that there is something beyond brand image – however widely defined – that can help us fill the gap. The new construct that I have identified and worked with, I call Brands' Attitudes.

Brands' Attitudes

The apostrophe in the term "brands' attitudes" is important, because it distinguishes it from the term "brand attitude" (no apostrophe), a term which is often used by consumer scientists as a synonym for brand image. The latter is not a very precise term, because what is actually meant by it is *consumers'* attitudes – toward the brand; but it is out there, and I have to deal with it. My term – brands' attitude – on the other hand, describes exactly what it means; it describes consumers' perceptions of *brands'* beliefs, *brands'* desires, *brands'* intentions. A brand has an attitude inasmuch as the consumer ascribes *intentionality* to it, and the brand's attitude is the consumer's projection of the brand's "self-awareness." The fact that the two constructs – brand image and brands' attitudes – are both consumer perceptions or projections does not mean that they are the same; everything that concerns us "lives" in the consumer's mind, but what I am distinguishing are two separate dimensions of consumers' perceptions which are very different in kind. The following real-life cases will serve to introduce the new construct of Brands' Attitudes and to illustrate its importance.

1. The American Express Card

The American Express brand of T&E (Travel and Entertainment) charge card was not the first in that category; that honor belongs to the Diners Card, which American Express effectively eclipsed. Nor did it have greater functionality than other "plastic" – the original lack of a revolving credit facility and the narrower range of outlets where it was accepted were vulnerabilities which its credit card competitors, such as Visa, were quick to exploit. The brand was successfully and purposively built on a prestige platform, by associating it with a variety of well-known people – among them prominent politicians and top sports and show-business celebrities. The "Do you know me?" advertising campaign, which played through the first half of the 1980s, has become one of the classics.

Figure 1.1 shows data from a mid 1990s brand image survey; at that time, American Express had nearly a three to one advantage, in terms of prestige, over all of its credit card competitors, and a substantial edge over Diners, its only T&E competitor.

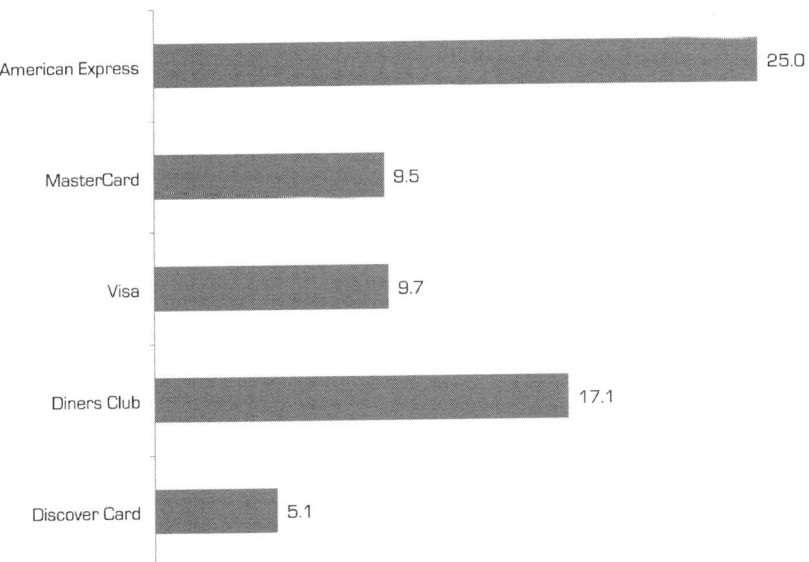

FIGURE 1.1   Credit Cards' Prestige Image

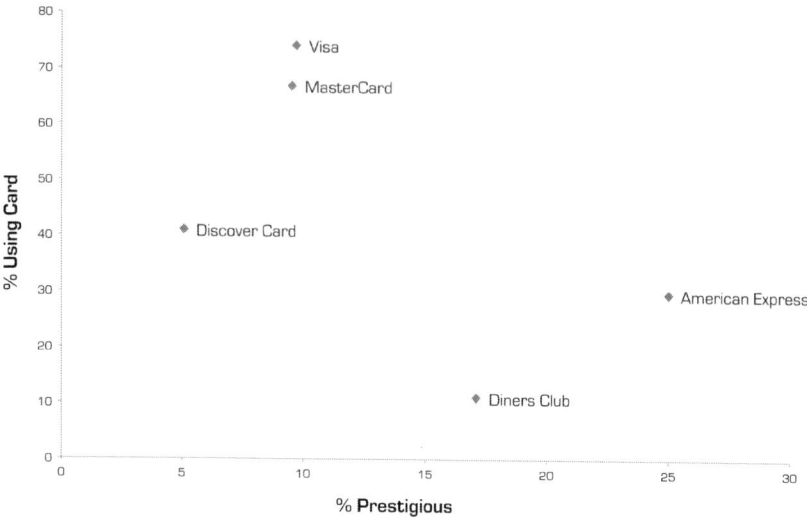

FIGURE 1.2 Credit Card Use and Prestige Image

If prestige was the core element of the American Express brand image, that should mean that its far greater prestige would have won it more users – i.e. holders of the American Express Card – than other cards. However, Figure 1.2, showing the relationship between perceptions of prestige and card ownership from the same data set as Figure 1.1, seems to demonstrate almost exactly the opposite.

This is, of course, a case of "correlation without causation," but it does at least raise a question about the relevance of prestige to the Amex image. The topic of prestige is the whole subject of Chapter 4; suffice it to point out here that prestige might be an ideal image platform for a brand targeted at an elite group – as was originally the case with the American Express Card. But it clearly has limitations when – as was the case from about the mid 1980s – Amex management had decided to build an Amex brand architecture in which the iconic Green Card, the stand-ard-bearer of the brand, was tasked with becoming a mass-market offering. The resistance that the Green Card met to the expansion of its franchise made it look as though prestige was possibly an obstacle to the growth of the brand, rather than a platform that enabled it. Fortunately, before such a conclusion was reached, we looked at the relationship between card ownership and another set of perceptions – relating to the descriptor "Unapproachable." This is shown in Figure 1.3.

Here it is clear that the more a credit card brand is seen as unapproachable the less likely it is to be used. This looked more like the real barrier that American Express had to overcome.

The difference between prestigious and unapproachable is that prestigious is an *attribute* – presumably a desirable attribute – of the brand, whereas unapproachable is an *attitude* – presumably *un*desirable – of the brand; prestigious is a dimension of brand image – the consumer's attitude toward the brand; unapproachable is

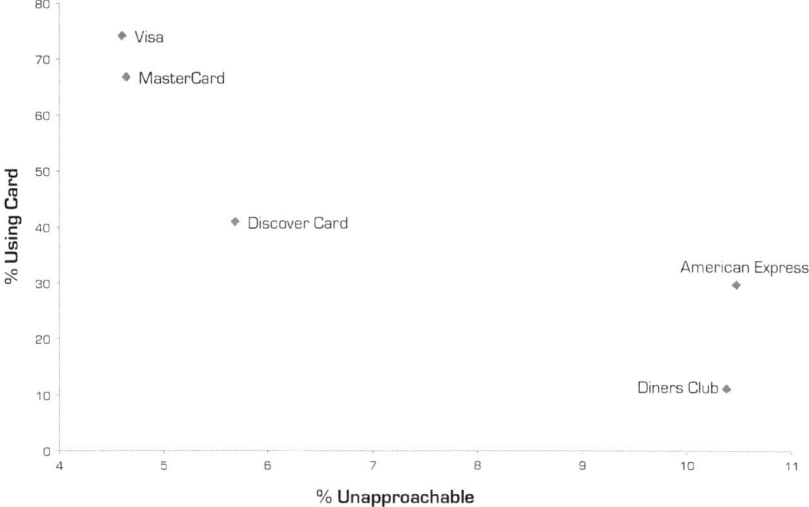

FIGURE 1.3   Credit Card Use and Unapproachable Brand's Attitude

something qualitatively different – it is a characteristic of the "brand's attitude" toward the consumer. What does it mean to be unapproachable? Think about how you would characterize an unapproachable person; that person would tend to rebuff or resist contact with you, would give you the impression that they did not want to have anything to do with you, perhaps did not consider you sufficiently worthy to associate with. What if you thought that a credit card – particularly one that refers to its card holders as "members" – didn't really want you as one of its holders? Would you go ahead and get it anyway because it is prestigious? Or would your attitude be "who needs prestige!"?

The problem for American Express – and for other brands that wish to appear prestigious – is that being prestigious and being unapproachable often do tend to go together. Figure 1.4 shows the relationship between these two perceptions for 48 US brands, from eight different product categories. The scales for both measures have been normalized in order to be able to compare their distributions; the axes intersect at the average point of each.

There is a weak positive correlation between the two – more prestigious brands do *tend* to be seen as more unapproachable – but the connection is by no means inevitable. Whereas all the brands in the top right-hand sector of the chart are above average on both prestige and unapproachable, the brands in the bottom right-hand sector are above average on prestige *but below average for unapproachable*. In fact, exactly half of the brands that are above average on prestige are below average on unapproachable.

What this means is that it is possible to be seen as prestigious without alienating potential users with an off-putting brand attitude – but it takes work. Crucially,

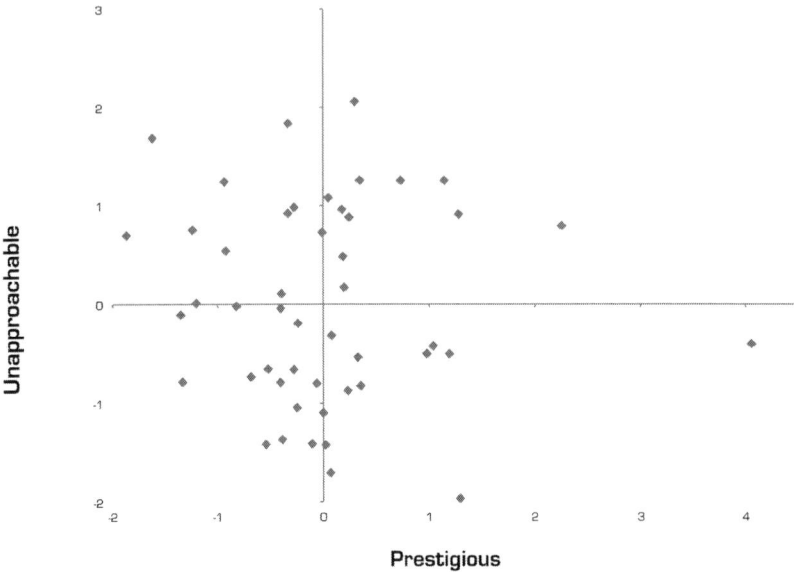

FIGURE 1.4 Prestige Image vs Unapproachable Brands' Attitude

it means that you cannot just manage brand image – consumers' attitudes; you have to take just as much care of the brand's attitudes too. The study on the relationships of the American Express brands with different segments of credit card users, from which this data was abstracted, made it very clear what was holding back the brand's expansion; it was not that the brand was too prestigious, but too unapproachable. In Chapter 4, which deals specifically with relationships with prestige and luxury brands, I will explain how the brand tackled this attitude problem, and how effective that action proved to be.

2. Casual Dining Restaurants

For most casual dining choices, the touchstones of brand image are quality and good value. For restaurants, quality is a multi-faceted factor, reflecting the quality of service and the whole eating experience, as well as the quality of the food itself; value for money is "computed" against this complex of quality issues. In this fiercely competitive category, many diners regularly patronize a number of different brands of restaurant; and, although they have preferences between the brands, loyalty – in the sense of patronizing only one brand – hardly exists. The key objective is therefore not just to maximize the number of diners that use your brand, but to maximize the share of regular diners' eating occasions that your brand gets. Quality and value are important in this but – because they are so basic – they represent just cost of entry into this category; if a casual dining brand cannot convince potential customers of its quality and value, then it will not even reach the first hurdle; and if it does, these two factors alone will not provide it with the competitive leverage that it needs to build share of eating occasions and dollar share. In studies of this category – and other food-related categories – I have found that there is a third factor that is much more likely to lead to brand preference than just quality or value; that factor is a measure of the extent to which consumers see the brand as "worth more than it costs." Figure 1.5 shows the relationship between each of these three factors – quality, value and worth more – and brand preference. The data is from a 2012 survey, carried out by my consultancy, based on a sample of casual dining restaurant chain customers (men and women).

Each of the points represents the "score" of each of six casual dining brands for two measures – the percentage of diners saying that they prefer the restaurant (vertical axis) and the percentage attributing either quality, value, or being worth more to that brand (horizontal axis).

There is, as we might expect, a strong connection between higher attribution on each of the factors and brand preference; working from left to right, Friendly's and Denny's get the lowest level of attribution on each of the three factors; Olive Garden and Outback Steakhouse generally get the highest. In terms of brand preference, the order is the same, with Denny's and Friendly's the lowest and Outback Steakhouse the highest. For each of the three factors, the points lie more or less along a straight line. The relative strength of the connection between each factor and brand preference can be seen by comparing the slopes of the three trend lines; the steeper the slope of the trend line, the more

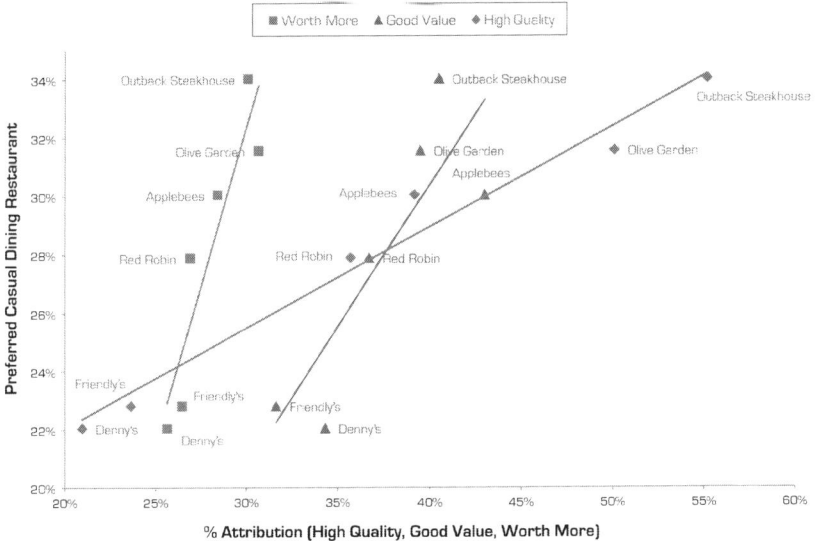

FIGURE 1.5   Correlates of Preference for Casual Dining Chain

highly that factor is correlated with brand preference. The Good Value line is steeper than the High Quality line, and the Worth More line is steeper still than that; Worth More is much more highly correlated with brand preference than the other two factors.

Being "worth more" thus appears to be a very strong influence on diners' preference for casual dining restaurants; what exactly does that mean and how does it differ from "good value"? Again I would argue that the difference is between a brand's attribute and a brand's attitude; value is an *attribute* of the brand, the result of comparing quality with price. "Worth more," on the other hand, reflects an *attitude* of the brand, a willingness to give more than it takes. How would you describe a person who gives more than they take? Selfless, giving of themselves – generous? In a very literal sense, a restaurant that gives very generous servings or throws in extras for no cost could be said to be displaying a generous, "worth more" attitude. But in a broader sense, generosity is a key attitude for all food and food-related brands; food is a source of nourishment – for the individual and for the group or family; the archetypal source of nourishment is the mother with her selfless attitude toward her child. Successful brands in any food or food-related category therefore need to project some "motherhood"; they need to go above and beyond – they need to be "worth more." Whether we define the brand's attitude as motherhood or just generosity, it is crucial. In Chapter 3 we will investigate in greater depth the case of another food brand in which a brand's generous attitude – or lack of such – was the core issue.

3. Women's Magazines

In a study among regular readers of eight leading women's magazines, readers were asked to imagine their favorite magazine as a person, and to answer two questions about this "person." First they had to pick, from a list of 40 personality characteristics, the three that best described the personality of their magazine. Figure 1.6 shows the percentage picking each of the magazines on five of the most important of these characteristics.

What is immediately noticeable is that the personalities of these magazines are generally very differentiated one from another; "Sexy" was picked to describe *Cosmopolitan* by nearly 50 percent of its readers, while the next highest to get this attribution was chosen by only 12 percent. *Us Weekly* and *People* were described as "Fun" and "Sociable" by much higher proportions of their readers than other magazines. The percentages of those picking "Stylish" to describe their magazine shows a marked differentiation between *Vogue* and *InStyle* at 100 percent, compared to 20 percent or less for *Cosmopolitan*, *Us Weekly*, and *People*. The brand positioning of the magazines, in personality terms, is very clear: *Cosmopolitan* owns sexy; *Us Weekly* and *People* own sociability; while *Vogue* and *InStyle* own stylish.

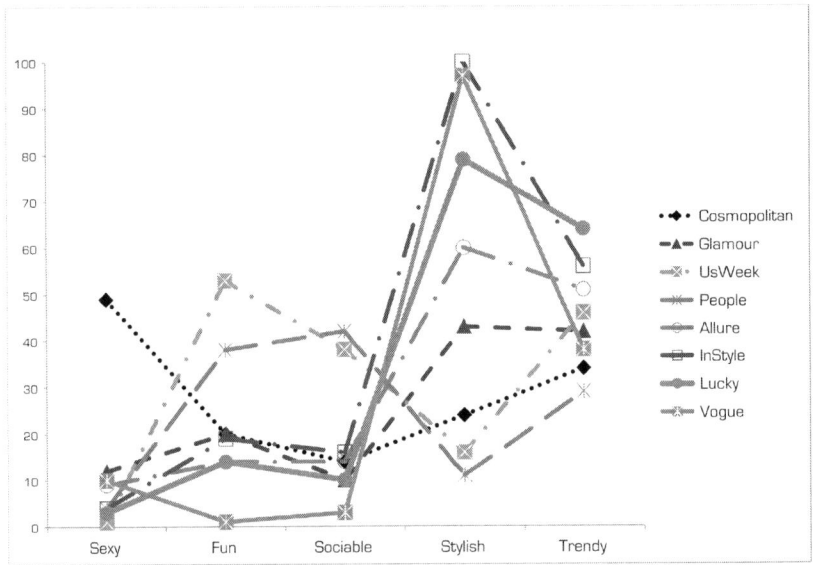

FIGURE 1.6 Magazines' Personality Profiles

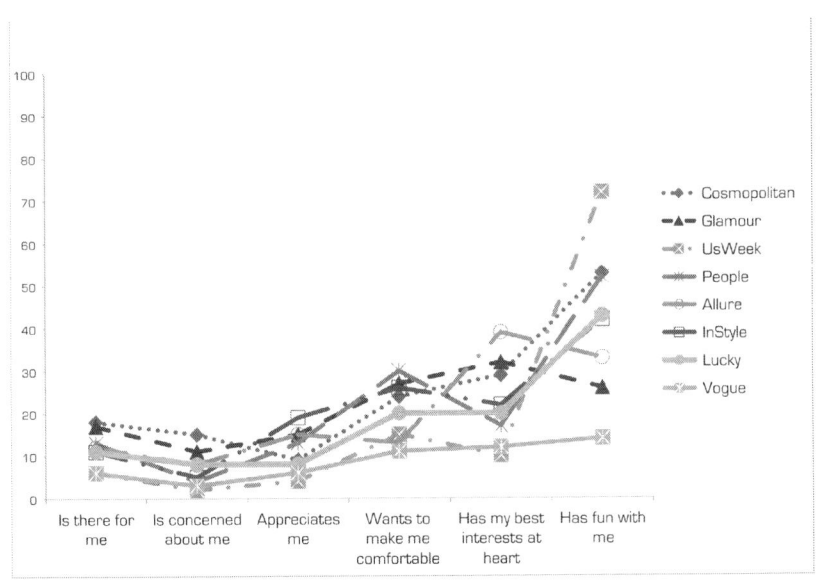

FIGURE 1.7 Magazines' Brands' Attitudes

Second, readers were asked to pick, from a list of 24 statements expressing how the magazine "person" feels about the reader, the three which best described the attitudes of their magazine toward them. Figure 1.7 shows the percentage picking each of the magazines on the six most differentiated of these brands' attitudes.

In contrast to the very distinct way in which readers were able to characterize the personality of their magazine, the picture with regard to the magazines' attitudes is far less clear. With the exception of *Allure* – which 40 percent of readers say "Has my best interests at heart" – and *US Weekly* – which does well on "Has fun with me" – the magazines are much less differentiated on these characteristics. There are no 100 percent selections, and hardly any 50 percent or 60 percent selections. Unlike with brand personality, the positioning space for brands' attitudes is up for grabs. What this means – with the exceptions mentioned above – is that readers really do not know how to describe their magazine's attitude toward them. The question is, does this matter? Is it not sufficient that a magazine has a clear brand personality?

Readers were also asked a series of questions designed to measure the extent of their loyalty to their magazine. In this category, loyalty translates to regular purchasing and readership; greater loyalty means a greater likelihood of picking the title out from the tens of others on a display. Even though the survey respondents were all – by definition – regular readers of each magazine, there was considerable variation in loyalty, which ranged from a high of 77 percent among readers of *Glamour* to a low of 57 percent among *Vogue* readers.

What is it about these magazines which gives rise to the different levels of attachment to them among their readers? Specifically, which of the characteristics associated with them – brand personality or brand attitudes – contribute the most? Figure 1.8 shows the ten items from both lists combined – brand personality and brands' attitudes – that correlate most highly with loyalty.

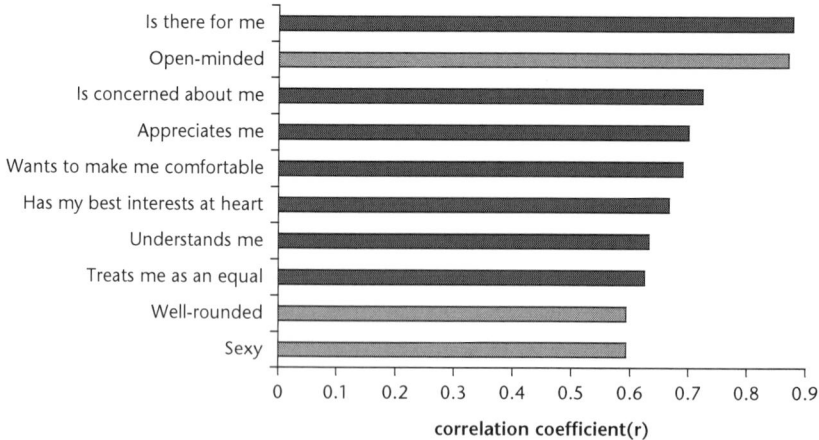

FIGURE 1.8 Women's Magazines – Top Ten Correlates of Loyalty

Brands' attitudes (black bars) account for seven of the top ten correlates with loyalty, and personality characteristics (grey bars) only for three. Of the top five – all of them with a correlation of over 0.6 – "Open-minded" is the only personality characteristic; all of the others are expressions of the brand's attitude toward the consumer.

So the answer to the question posed above – does it matter that readers cannot describe their magazines' attitude toward them? – is that it definitely does. By not clearly crafting an attitude toward their readers, these magazines are losing out on a potential competitive edge in the battle for readership and loyalty.

4. Corporate Brands and Social Issues

Brands at all levels are increasingly concerned about being perceived as good corporate citizens. "Green" marketing, "Cause-related marketing," and "Brand Socialization" are not just buzzwords in marketing departments; they are activities behind which many companies have harnessed considerable corporate resources and budgets. There is no doubt that their policies do make a tangible difference in the public sphere – whether it be in alleviating the "tragedy of the commons," addressing the needs of disadvantaged populations, or enhancing cultural and recreational life. The question is whether there is also a real pay-off in terms of corporate reputation.

A study conducted in Israel set out to try and construct an index of Brand Socialization. To this end, eight different corporate brands – two brands from each of four completely different categories (banks, supermarket chains, mobile phone operators, and food companies) – were rated on a series of dimensions. There were three groups of dimensions:

Corporate Brands' Attitudes, including statements such as:

- They know and understand their customers.
- They consider what their customers want.
- They treat their customers as equals.

Corporate Brands' Ethics, including statements such as:

- They act ethically and morally.
- They act lawfully.
- Their activities are transparent.
- Their advertising is truthful.
- They are concerned about the quality of the environment.

Corporate Brands' Philanthropy, including statements such as:

- They contribute to society and the public at large.
- They actively consider the future of society.

- They work hard to earn public trust.
- They are responsive to the needs of society and its organisms.
- They dedicate time and financial resources for the good of the community.

In addition, the brands were rated on a series of dimensions designed to measure their overall corporate reputation.

Figure 1.9 shows the brands' average scores for each group of dimensions (on the x axis), plotted against the brands' scores for corporate reputation (on the y axis).

It can be seen that for both corporate brand attitudes and corporate brand ethics there is a strong monotonic relationship between brands' perceived performance on these dimensions and their overall reputation. For corporate philanthropy, although there is a relationship between the two, it does not hold for all the brands. Clearly, spending on social marketing by Orange, Cellcom, and Bank Hapoalim is not translating through to enhanced corporate reputation in the same way it appears to for the other brands.

The other point to note is that for each one of the eight brands its point on the corporate ethics (lower) line is to the right of its point on the corporate brand attitudes (upper) line; in order to achieve a certain level of overall corporate brand reputation, corporate brands apparently "need" a greater reputation for ethics than they do for good attitude. I suspect that an ethical reputation is much easier to lose than it is to gain, and that corporate brands' attitudes may therefore be more manageable upwardly than are corporate ethics. There is an injunction in one of the Psalms to "avoid evil and do good"; they are not one and the same. Analogously, the ideal corporation reputation strategy might be to avoid doing the things that damage the brand's reputation for ethics, and to actively seek to do things that improve the corporate brand's attitude.

FIGURE 1.9 Correlates of Corporate Reputation

How you manage a corporate brand's attitudes may seem less intuitive than for the other types of brands I have discussed here. Chapter 6 is devoted entirely to this topic, but a short anecdote may help to introduce the idea. Some years ago, I was consulting with public utility companies who, in the wake of deregulation and the consequent loss of protected markets in the USA, were thinking – for the first time – about their corporate brands. Customer satisfaction studies showed that gas and electric companies' scores peaked in the aftermath of a recovery from natural disasters, like an earthquake or a power outage following a heavy winter storm. Disaster recovery – like ethics and corporate philanthropy – is a given, but it cannot substitute for training service center employees to answer the phone promptly and with a pleasant manner, or for training "hard hat" employees out in the street to keep their pants pulled up and to minimize inconvenience to the public, or for designing a customer-friendly bill; these are all typical components of the ongoing management of a corporate brand's attitudes. They may seem like service delivery issues – and at the operational level that is just what they are – but in the mind of the consumer they are expressions of underlying attitudes, of an intentionality – a set of beliefs, desires, and intentions – which they ascribe to the corporate brand.

Brand Love Is not Enough

I was originally going to give this book a title that just reflected the theoretical grounding of its topic. However, as I was revising a final draft, it occurred to me how frequently I have referred very critically to the currently popular concept of Brand Love. Today, the idea of "brand love" – by which is meant the *consumer's love for the brand* – is a very popular metric, and often seems to be the be-all and end-all of brand equity measures. Many academic careers, at least one major brand consultancy, and a large international advertising group all make their living on just this one brand concept. I have illustrated, with the previous examples in this chapter, that there are important consumer brand relationships that have nothing to do with brand love; but here I do want to focus on it, and pinpoint the major failing of current "brand love" concepts and practices. It is not enough to ask whether or how much the consumer loves the brand; it is essential to ask also whether the brand loves the consumer, and how it shows that love. The old line that "it takes two to tango" is as true of the relationship between a consumer and a brand as it is of that between two people. Unless there is some reciprocity in the relationship, unless the consumer's love for the brand is met with an appropriate emotional response, then the consumer's love remains unrequited.

In fact, brands can and do act in such a way that the consumer experiences their actions as an emotional response to their own; but many brands do not. In the surveys that I referred to earlier, in which we measured consumers' love for brands, we also measured the level of projected emotional response from brands to the consumer; we found that 37 percent of consumers in the USA and 27 percent in Mexico perceived no emotional response from the brands we asked them about. Even when we selected just the brands that consumers said that *they* loved or liked a lot, only about 50 percent of consumers in each country experienced a strong emotional response from these brands.

Below are more findings from these surveys, in order to illustrate that crafting the brand in such a way as to elicit an appropriate emotional response projection from the consumer is essential in order to maximize the returns on a branded business.

At the beginning of this chapter, I quoted the finding of our surveys; that about one in four of the people who never use a brand say they "love it" or "like it a lot." Figure 1.10 shows how the level of brands' emotional response helps explain this gap between brand love and brand usage.

In both countries, loved brands with a strong emotional response have more users than those with a weak emotional response; more importantly, the greater proportion of these additional users are those who prefer the brand.

Figure 1.11 shows that the level of brands' emotional response affects the price elasticity of the brand. Brands that love the consumer can command a higher price.

In our surveys, respondents were asked to describe their feeling about the price of brands – the brands they say they love or like a lot – by picking a point on a seven-point "pricing power" scale, in which the top, center, and bottom boxes are labeled as shown in the chart; the chart shows a summary, in which

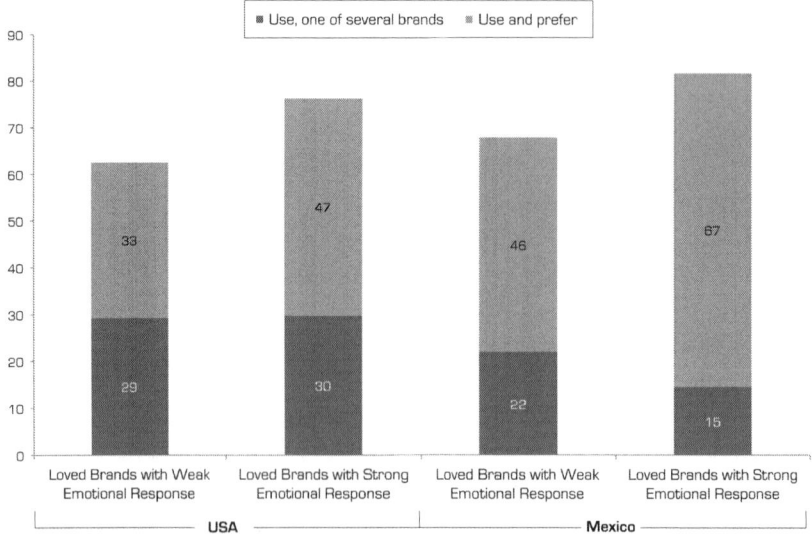

FIGURE 1.10 Use of and Preference for Loved Brands

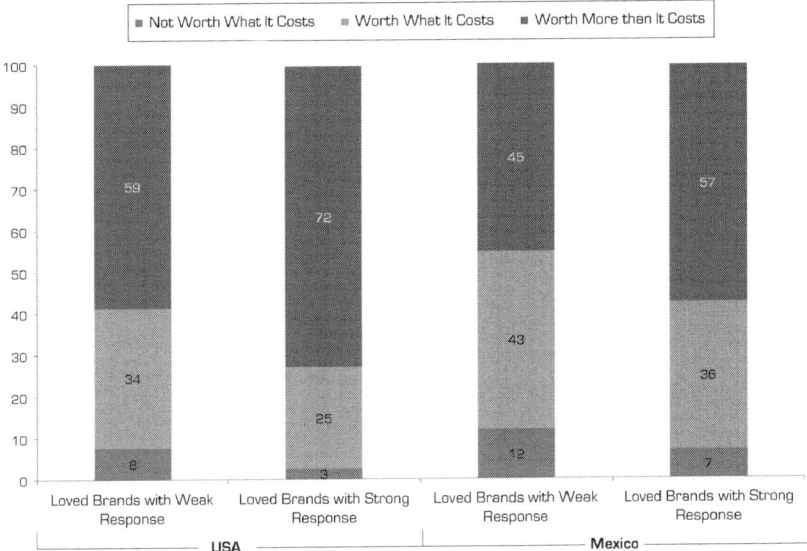

FIGURE 1.11   Pricing Power of Loved Brands

the seven points are collapsed into three. The level of emotional response of loved brands – weak or strong – makes a difference to the pricing power of brands; in both countries the percentage of respondents rating loved brands as worth more than they cost is 20–30 percent higher for those brands with a strong emotional response.

Increasingly, involvement with brands in social media is regarded as the touchstone of consumer brand relationships. Although my position is that consumer brand relationships are created in the consumer's mind and not in the media, the internet and social media clearly represent an important channel for their articulation and development. Figure 1.12 shows the effect that brands' emotional responses have on consumers' brand-related activities in social media.

In both countries the level of emotional response of loved brands makes a difference to the level of engagement with the brand in various social media activities. In particular, searching for it online, "liking" the brand, and recommending it to a friend are all substantially higher for loved brands that respond strongly to the consumer.

What I have tried to show in this chapter is that people really like brands enough to use them, prefer them, and become attached to them only if those brands seem to like *them*; conversely, people are much less likely to develop strong relationships with brands that appear indifferent to them; people reject brands that seem to them to be snooty or condescending. More generally, consumers cannot form *any* type of relationship – good or bad – with a brand unless they can ascribe intentionality to it. Consumers' relationships with brands

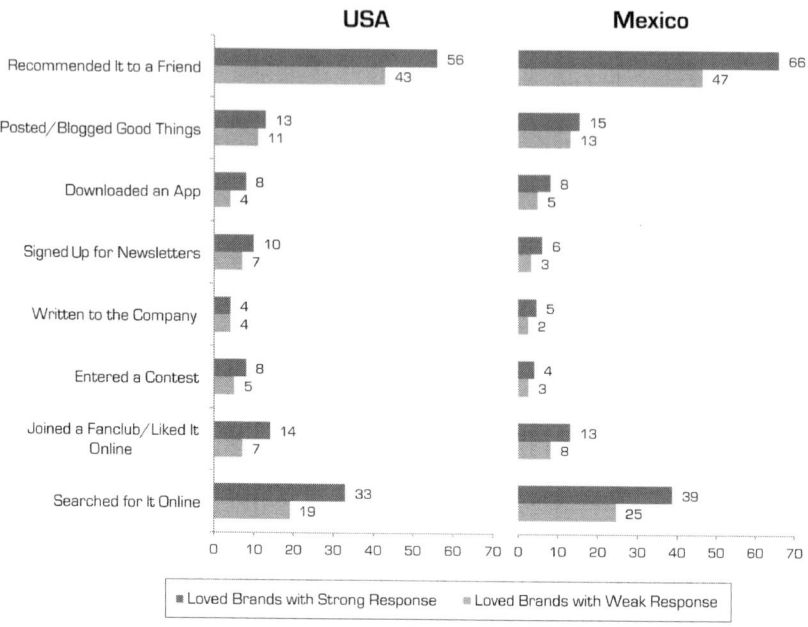

FIGURE 1.12 Social Media Activities with Loved Brands

depend not just on what they think of the brand but also on what the consumer believes that *the brand thinks*. The latter is what I call "brands' attitude"; it is every bit as real and influential as the attitudes that consumers have toward brands – brand image. Brands' attitudes – like brand images – of course exist only in the consumer's mind – but they are separate and distinct from brand images, and should be given the same level of attention that marketing people normally give to developing an effective brand image. The brands' attitude concept in fact provides an additional set of tools for the marketer, which complements the traditional one of brand image. In the next chapter I will take a temporary step back from the market to give a fuller and more comprehensive description of the theory of brands' attitudes, the theory I call Relational Branding.

2

THE RELATIONAL BRAND

"No man is an island/Entire of itself." The much-quoted lines from John Donne remind us of the interconnectedness of all human experience, that true independence can be at best a momentary illusion. According to the relational school of psychology, this is the case not just in the observable world of inter-personal relationships, but also in the interior world of the mind. According to relational thinking, external relationships – with other people and with things – are paralleled by psychic representations of these relationships within the mind. External relationships – those relationships that happen in the social world – thus have a pervasive effect on our psychic development; correspondingly, our internal psychic representations of others – fantasies – have equally pervasive effects in shaping our external relationships and relational behavior in "real" life.

"The profound significance of relational psychology is that it deals with rela-tions not only between external people and things, but also between and among internal personifications and representations."[1] Relational Branding – based on the insights of relational psychology – uses this additional "dimension" of meaning to gain a fuller understanding of the way consumers relate to brands. Figure 2.1 shows a symbolic representation of the parallel realms of the relational brand.

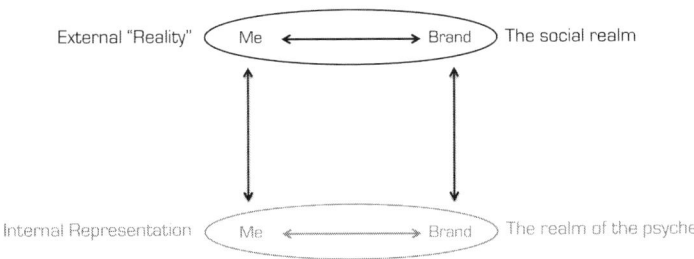

FIGURE 2.1 The Relational Brand – First Draft

In fact, the parallel between "internal" and "external" is not quite as simple as it is illustrated in Figure 2.1. We need to take a short excursion into the world of the developing infant mind, in order to refine our understanding of the world of internal representations of brands.

Stages in the Development of the Relational Personality

Relational psychology identifies these three stages in the early development of personality.

Transitional experiencing occurs at a point in the infant's development between the early emergence of consciousness – when the infant has no concept of things outside of herself/himself – and the infant's growing awareness of otherness. At this point in psychic development, there exists in the infant mind no clear distinction between what is "me" and what is "other" – such as the mother, the breast, or the feeding bottle.

"The core of transitional experiencing has to do with an inherent fit between the infant's creativeness and the world – a fit that is lived and taken for granted. The baby creates the object, but the object was there waiting to be created. The transitional object carries the meaning of that which is – yet is not – mother and that which is – and is not – self. It, like mother, mirrors the self and like the self, mirrors mother. Yet it cannot be reduced to either."[2]

D. W. Winnicott, the "father" of relational psychology, liked to say: "There is no such thing as an infant – only the infant-mother unit." The important point he was making was that this unit – the infant's primal and prototypical relationship has emergent properties, properties that transcend the individuality of the two participants. The infant at this stage has no perception of the object's distinct meaning outside of that combined unit.

At a later stage of development – *object relating* – the infant has to allow certain alterations in the self to take place. The "other" has now become meaningful in and of itself, and the infant is depleted, to the extent that something that s/he had up to now perceived as a part of him/herself is now found in the object. "The development of psychic structure begins with this basic self-identification, which includes relatedness to and aspects of the other, and it continues through internalizations and splitting-off of internalized self-other representations to create an inner world consisting of different aspects of an 'I' in relation to different aspects of the other."[3]

At a later (and ultimate) phase of development, known as *object usage*, the other is recognized as totally external, but because of the way the person has "learned" to relate to others, relationships are always built in that transitional space where self and "other" interact. Relationships thus constitute an integral part of the personality, which is in fact a "composite structure, formed and built up out of countless never-ending influences and exchanges between ourselves and 'others.' These 'others' – people and things – therefore effectively form parts of our own personality – not the whole of them, but such parts or aspects of them that we related to"[4] – and that process of *putting self in others and others in self* continues throughout life.

This is how relational psychology fundamentally reformulates the concept of self, in terms of personality development; but how does the brand fit into this picture?

The transitional space is not just the incubator for relationships with other people, it is also where objects – such as blankets, comforters, and brands – are related to, in order to provide support, create intimacy, and fulfill ludic (play) needs; there, relationships with these objects are created via the same relational process of putting self in others and others in self. The insight of relational psychology is that these inanimate relationship partners – so-called "Transitional Objects" – may be invested with the same type of characteristics – personality, motivations, attitudes, etc. – as animate ones. We have already seen in Chapter 1 several examples of consumers relating to brands as if they have attitudes. There, I used the word *intentionality* when referring to the ascription of attitudes to the brand; intentionality is a psychological construct, which means the ability to represent or give meaning to something. There are progressive "orders" of intentionality; first-order intentionality is the ability to represent something in one's own mind, to have self-awareness; second-order intentionality is the ability to represent something that exists in another person's mind, to be able to make sense of statements like: "I believe he thinks that." In the jargon, this is referred to as having a "theory of mind" about someone other than oneself. Having a theory of mind is fundamental to all relationships; one of the common hypotheses about why autistic people have difficulty with relationships is that they have failed to develop a theory of mind about other people. Only if we can form a belief about another person's intentional state can we know whether to trust them, whether to act with commitment toward them, whether to respect them, etc. Without a "theory of mind" about a brand, the consumer cannot form a true relationship with it; only a brand to which the consumer is able to ascribe beliefs, desires, and intentions is capable of being trusted, committed to or respected. The relational brand has intentionality, because the consumer relates to it *as if the brand itself has self-awareness*. It is this that makes the relational brand a Transitional Object, a legitimate participant in that inner space of the mind where relationships are created.

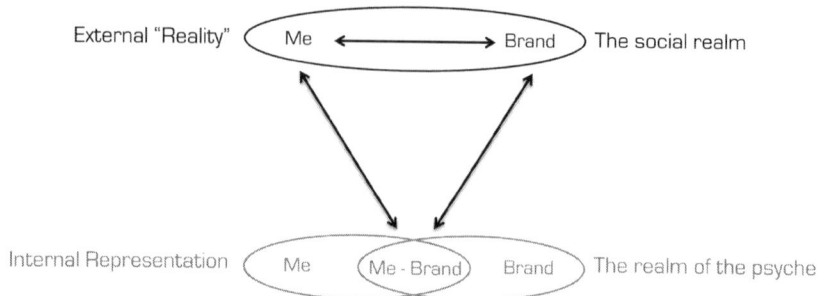

FIGURE 2.2　The Relational Brand – Second Draft

So, we can now reformulate the visual representation of the consumer/brand relationship as in Figure 2.2.

The Relational Brand vs the Freudian "Driven" Brand

The Relational Brand is clearly not the same as the brand of conventional consumer psychology, which is still largely in thrall to traditional Freudian psychology. The latter emphasizes the importance of innate "drives" – sexuality, aggression, etc. – in the understanding of the psyche and its influence on behavior. Drive theories, however, preserve a very fixed and absolutist view of these personality attributes. They do not allow for how such attributes may take on other meanings depending on the context or the relationship. In a relationship there is an interaction between two sets of attributes – the personalities of each of its participants; the nature of the relationship – and its influence on behavior – is clearly derived from the separate personalities of the two participants, but it is not simply reducible to either. A relationship has *emergent* qualities, meaning that it may be more – or less – than the sum of the parts. The Freudian "driven" brand is always the same, irrespective of the nature of its consumer-partner; the relational brand, on the other hand, is defined also by that relational process of putting others in self and self in others, by its interactions with the consumer.

Why Relational Branding ?

The emphasis on "brand drivers" of conventional consumer psychology has led to a cumbersome process of brand positioning, in which consumers' needs have to be matched up with brands' attributes. The weakness in this approach has always been the question of what mechanism to adopt for matching brand attributes with consumer needs. Anyone who has ever used a computer dating service will be aware of the problem. Just because the computer has determined that person A shares a lot of interests, preferences, and prejudices with person B, it does not guarantee that the latter will turn out to be person A's heart's desire – or he/she theirs. What is required, in order to make a good match, is a "match-making psychology" – an algorithm which incorporates a knowledge of the basic chemistry of relationships, and an understanding of the possible reactions and interactions that can occur between the two. Relational Branding makes this process much easier, by working in the opposite direction; Relational Branding starts by defining the relationship itself, and then *inferring* from this starting point the brand attributes and consumer personality attributes necessary to sustain that relationship. As in most areas of scientific enquiry, it is much easier to deconstruct a higher-order, more complex phenomenon into its component elements than to try and synthesize it from the components.

So, the relational solution can be both a shortcut to brand positioning as well as offering the best chance of getting a good fit between the chosen positioning and the needs of the target consumer. Relational Branding turns the conventional process on its head; it starts at the end-point, by identifying, from the set of possible relationships, those which are most desirable, and then – via inference – determines which consumer needs and which brand benefits are required for this relationship. Because the process is goal-oriented – it looks for certain types of relationship – the information requirements are less, and the processing of the information is simpler – algorithmic rather than heuristic.

What then is the methodology of Relational Branding? It is implicit that it has to be based on the psychology of relationships, and this means that it has to work at the level of the single case – the single brand-consumer dyad – before it can be generalized to whole target groups and populations. This disaggregated requirement gives the relational approach a precision and focus that can be lacking in the conventional approach – in which both consumers' needs and brand benefits are often already expressed as statistical averages or aggregates, with the consequent opportunity for error compounding error into meaninglessness.

Relational Branding Methodology

Conventionally, interactions between the brand and the consumer are treated as if they take place in an "external" objective reality; each party has its own "internal" world, which determines a set of attitudes and behaviors – the consumer's psyche driving his needs and purchasing behavior, the brand's marketing milieu determining its positioning and marketing activities. But these two "internal" worlds are seen as insulated from each other, only interacting at the level of the attitudes and behavior that they give rise to. Relational Branding recognizes that the consumer and brand share an "internal" space – which happens to be in the consumer's mind – in which the *precursors* to attitudes and behaviors of each interact and are co-determined.

In order to develop a methodology for both identifying and prescribing consumers' relationships with brands, it is necessary to shift the focus away from the "external" world in which the separate attributes of the consumer and the brand interact, to the relational space in consumers' minds in which the brand-self is formed. Clearly, we cannot enter this space or observe it directly, but we can infer something about it by observing the external effects it has on the two parties – brand and consumer. The principal effects we can observe are attitudes and behaviors – the attitudes and behaviors of the consumer toward the brand, and *the attitudes and behavior of the brand.*

This is no different from the way we draw conclusions about the relationship between two people. Although we are unable to see into the transitional space of either, we can infer the nature of the relationship between two people by observing the attitudes and behaviors they display toward each other. Unless they are involved in play-acting, an experienced analyst will be able to make some fairly accurate inferences.

Figure 2.3 illustrates a thought experiment concerning a hypothetical relationship between a doctor and a patient.

If we let the doctor stand in for the brand, the characteristics on the left constitute the patient's attitude toward the doctor – the patient's perception of the doctor's "brand personality." He's highly skilled, caring, and funny – sounds like a doctor we would all like to have, and we would expect the patient to like the doctor.

Figure 2.4, however, gives us the full story.

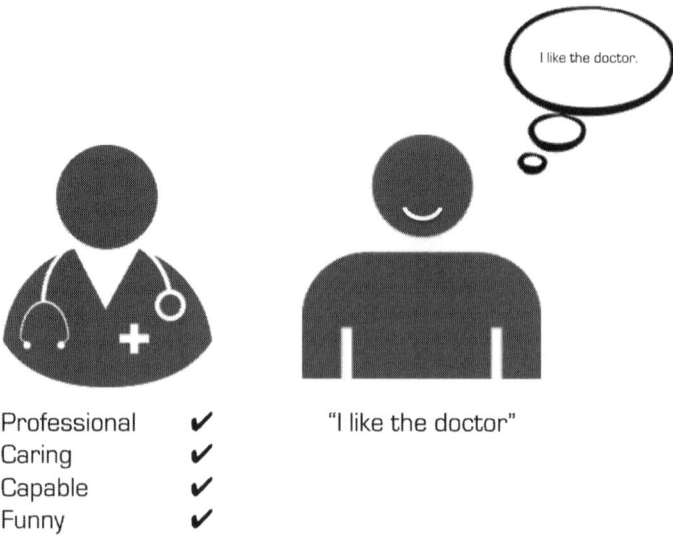

FIGURE 2.3   The Doctor–Patient Relationship 1

Professional ✔

Caring ✔

Capable ✔

Funny ✔

"I don't like the doctor"

FIGURE 2.4   The Doctor–Patient Relationship 2

When we uncover the crucial bit of information about what the patient believes the doctor thinks of him – that he is a hypochondriac – our understanding of the nature of the relationship changes completely. And it doesn't matter what the doctor really thinks because, for the patient, the relationship is based on what *he* believes about the doctor's attitude.

Just as the doctor in the patient's mind is not co-identical with an objective descriptive reality of the doctor, so the brand in the consumer's mind is an internal representation not co-identical with any objective description of the "real" brand. (In fact, unlike the doctor, the brand in many ways lacks any reality.) It is necessary that we make this shift in our perspective – from thinking about the brand as something external to the consumer, to thinking about the brand as essentially in the consumer's mind. As David Ogilvy famously said: "A brand is the consumer's *idea* of a product." (My italics.) The managers of brands have become very skilled at manipulating just one aspect of these internal representations of brands – brand image; they have created, via mass communications, consensus representations of brands, such that whole groups of consumers share the same – or very similar – representations. This is what has permitted us to talk about brand image and brand personality, as if they were external realities that we control. We know what the consumer believes about the brand; but the question that has gone unanswered – indeed unasked – is: "What does the *consumer believe* that the brand thinks?"

What the doctor–patient interaction is meant to illustrate is that there are two distinct aspects to the consumer's internal representation of the brand, and it is the interaction between these two that defines the brand relationship. I have used the psychology of human relationships in order to illustrate the brand rela-tionships concept, because relational psychology enables us to apply the same "rules" to all transitional objects. It is not my purpose – even were I qualified – to delve much further into the psychology of human relationships, but there is a useful "reality check" we can do by focusing the argument back on humans. If brands' attitudes exist as a real construct, then we should be able to "retro-fit" the same construct to human relationships. Taking a "brand's eye" view of a human relationship means analyzing the relationship from the point of view of just one of the parties, and trying to understand it just from that perspective.

Take love, for example. What is it that turns admiration, respect, desire into that altogether different phenomenon that we call love? One answer is that being the *object* of someone else's love is the catalyst; true love blossoms when the mind's eye sees the potentially loved-one as reciprocating that sublime emotion. If the lover does not see – correctly or mistakenly – that same emotion recipro-cated, then love is soon blighted and eventually extinguished by the bitterness of a perceived rejection.

It is the facility to create internal representations of another person which also allows people to have intense relationships with someone they have never actually met – like a celebrity (celebrities – in terms of fans' relationships with them – are actually much more like brands than real people). In addition to the public image of these figures, there is also an inner representation – otherwise known as a fan-tasy – in the mind of each fan, a personally-animated version of the celebrity who knows and thinks about – and maybe loves – them too. Usually, the fantasy is well under conscious control, but we are all unfortunately too familiar with what can happen when the representation becomes the reality, and the person concerned starts to act on the basis of the imagined feelings of the celebrity toward them.

In other – less intense – relationships, how often have we felt antipathy or dislike toward people with thoroughly admirable qualities, who have never done anything to merit the lack of affection we feel toward them? Could it be that we are attributing to these people uncharitable feelings or unfavorable opinions about ourselves? These perceptions may reflect how we are feeling about ourselves at that time, and the person concerned is merely acting as a "mouthpiece" for self-criticism in our own minds. Alternatively, why are we sometimes fond of people who have what are generally regarded as "negative" qualities or poor values? Could it be because we imagine that they admire or respect – even envy – our good points, thereby increasing our own self-respect? If we were to behave consistently with our own values and reject them on the basis of theirs, then their imagined respect for us could have no possible worth.

The Objective and the Subjective Brand

There are two points that I hope to have established with these examples. The first is that the stage on which a relationship – with another person or with a brand – plays, is in the mind of one party to that relationship. To be sure, the relationship is open to external influence by the other party, but the "party of the first part" retains tight directorial control, ensuring that anything that occurs "off-stage" is filtered via and interpreted by the mind's eye. Second, all relationships result from the interaction of two independent mental constructs – between the "objective" characteristics of the second party and the attitudes imputed to them. Although both are part of the consumer's internal representation of the brand, it is useful for historical reasons to think of the first as the "objective" brand – because we have generally objectified the image of the brand – and the second, the brand's attitudes toward the consumer, as the "subjective" brand. Here is a definition of the two types of attitudes.

- The objective brand consists of the set of associations, images, and personality characteristics around which there is more or less a consensus. They represent the common or "public" meaning of the brand, in the sense that most people who know the brand – to a greater or lesser degree – share the same perceptions. For example, for most of us the name Kraft evokes ideas of quality, family, middle America. Nike means personal achievement, going for it, not accepting limitations. Apple means mold-breaking, creating new paradigms, being anti-establishment. The "objective" brand is the net impression left in the consumer's mind of all of the ideas, associations, and messages which have been systematically projected at the consumer about the brand. The "objective" brand is the brand that generally has been created by brand management.
- Brands' attitudes are a manifestation of the "subjective" brand. They are the consumer's beliefs about what the brand "wants," "thinks" or "feels" and how these "motivate" its behavior. Brands' attitudes may be generalized – like being unapproachable – or they may be personalized – "it is not interested in me." Brands' attitudes can be inferences made by the consumer about the brand's beliefs, feelings, and desires; they can also be projections of how the brand behaves so as to create specific experiences for the consumer. These have rarely been purposively managed, even though they represent a distinct and separate construct in the consumer's mind.

There is a danger in managing just the "objective" brand and not the "subjective" brand. Because consumers' relationships with a brand are the result of the interaction of the objective and subjective characteristics, the appropriate brand's attitude can help create a strong relationship; but if a brand has a "bad" or inappropriate attitude, then no amount of emphasis on its good image qualities can make up for that – it may even make the relationship worse. There are many examples of how "bad" attitudes – usually unmanaged brands' attitudes – can undermine the image of a brand, and lead to poor brand relationships. It is time to take a preliminary look at some of the brands' attitudes – good and bad – that we shall encounter in the later chapters.

High brand awareness is generally regarded as a prerequisite of a strong brand relationship; no less important is the brand equivalent – high consumer awareness. A consumer-aware brand creates a sense of involvement or intimacy with the consumer. The consumer believes that the brand is interested in knowing who the consumer is; the brand is able to demonstrate that interest via insight into the consumer's needs and empathy with the consumer's concerns. Consumer awareness matters for the same reason that brand awareness matters – to create an individual identity for the object of that awareness. Most people dislike being made to feel anonymous, indistinguishable parts of a faceless mass, so brands – even mass-market brands – have to find a way of addressing each consumer *as if* personally. This applies to all brands, but particularly to brand leaders. If a brand is acknowledged as a leader in its category and it is consumer-aware, this will result in a relationship in which the brand is admired and respected – like a role model or "mentor." This type of relationship often applies to brands that have dominated their product category, which have been innovators and leaders, or to brands which have just been around for a long time. Brand leaders must work hard to maintain their sense of interest in and involvement with the consumer. If they allow themselves to seem aloof or disinterested, their dominance may work against them. Instead of authoritative, the brand may be seen just as authoritarian; instead of respecting the brand, the consumer may begin to resent it. Brands that want respect – by leadership and innovation in their category – must also work to create links with their consumers – to make the consumer feel that by allying him or herself with the brand the consumer too becomes a leader.

Prestige brands must have "aspirational" images – recognized either for their outstanding quality and performance or for their elevated and generally desirable social connotations. Sometimes – like the proverbial Rolls-Royce – the brand will have both types of prestige qualifications. It is clear, however, that these qualities by themselves do not make a brand relationship. In addition to being desirable in and of itself, the consumer has to believe that the brand desires a relationship with the consumer; it must – like the old aristocrats who bestowed their patronage on commoners in return for services rendered – demonstrate its willingness to confer the benefits of its prestige on the consumer. Generally, people buy a prestige brand in order to enhance their self-esteem; so the last thing they need is to be made to feel inferior. This is the rub. In order to maintain the values that make them aspirational, these brands have to keep hitting all the appropriate "buttons" – prestige, status, exclusivity. In doing so, they risk appearing intimidating, snotty, and condescending to some consumers. Groucho Marx said that he would not join a club that wanted him as a member, but it takes a very strong ego to want to join a club that *doesn't* want you as a member, so people will reject a brand that they feel might reject them.

A brand can appear to want to take responsibility away from the consumer, either in a very protective and nurturing manner, or with a kind of professional "leave it to me" attitude. In certain categories – provided that the brand has the reputation and the performance to match its promise – this can lead to a very strong brand relationship. However, there are pitfalls; the consumer may simply not want a "super brand" level of performance, or may wish to be more involved in the task themselves, or may take offense at the implied attitude to his or her own competence. Many brands – among them most notably financial service brands – flaunt their sophistication, superior know-how, and unequaled expertise. But if their claims to being smarter, more advanced, and more savvy than all of their competitors result in the consumer believing that the brand thinks they are helpless and stupid, then the brand relationship will be fatally flawed. In contrast to this "brand knows best" attitude, the brand may seem to go out of its way to validate the consumer; by recognizing and respecting the consumer's autonomy, it emphasizes the consumer's competence and abilities rather than its own; by reflecting the consumer's self-image rather than interjecting its own, it plays back and amplifies the consumer's identity. This attitude is more appropriate when people wish to use a brand as a means of expressing their own individuality.

There are many brands – often the most well-known and veteran brands in a category – that consumers say they "can rely on." Too often the reality is that it is the brand that relies on the consumer – on the consumer's continued loyalty, on the consumer's passivity and unchanging requirements, on the consumer's willingness not to expect more. If this was ever a viable attitude for a brand, it is certainly destined to failure nowadays. Consumers do not want to feel taken for granted; they wish to feel appreciated. "We know you have a choice" is a sentiment that should not just be confined to an airline's farewell to its de-planing passengers. Frequent shopper and other loyalty programs may be the most tangible expression of an attitude of appreciation for the consumer but, as they become the norm, consumers need to be made to know in other ways too.

A brand may seem to be very supportive of the consumer, and to make efforts to try and "listen to" the consumer in order to understand and anticipate the consumer's needs. Brands that don't listen are seen as self-centered, concerned with their own needs to the exclusion of the consumer's. The more objectively successful the brand is, the more proactive its consumer marketing, the more critical it is that the subjective brand be perceived as focused on the needs of the consumer – not its own. The feelings of intimidation or disdain many people experience when faced by an aggressive sales person are the result of the perception that the latter is only pushing his or her own agenda. These same perceptions can easily be communicated by a brand.

Generosity is often a critical attitude of the brand. By definition, a healthy relationship requires give and take – by both parties; however, the taking – the satisfaction of each party's needs – may often eclipse the giving. In a brand relationship, the consumer gives money, commitment, and loyalty to the brand – and sometimes a lot more. People entrust the safety of their own or family members' health to brands of non-prescription medications; people put their reputation and self-respect on the line when they make big-ticket brand choices – either for themselves or on behalf of the businesses they represent. But even when the consumer's risk is only at the level of not getting a good-tasting cup of coffee, or feeling dissatisfied with a portion size, they will feel a lot more satisfied, a lot more rewarded in the relationship, if the brand seems to be acting generously toward them.

These are some of the ways in which the qualities of the brand relationship are influenced by the construct that I have defined as brands' attitudes. In the next section I define a more formal model, which describes how conceptually brands' attitudes interact with consumers' attitudes to determine the brand relationship.

The Relational Brand Model

There are and have been many approaches to modeling the influence of brand image on consumers' brand choices, including fairly complex models, based either on statistical algorithms or on decision theory. However, most practitioners have followed the principle of scientific parsimony – to be only as complicated as really necessary – and have opted for some version of the "additive" model. Essentially, this assumes that a brand's equity is the sum of its parts – and the modeling therefore consists of correctly identifying those parts, and determining the extent of their influence. One key assumption of all additive models is that a brand's strengths can in theory compensate for its weaknesses – in fact the additive "rule" is known in some circles as the "compensatory rule." The Relational Brand model departs from the additive assumption, because relationships are composed of two essentially different components, which interact in a non-compensatory manner. So the difference between those components must therefore be systematically preserved in a way that allows for more variegated forms of interaction than simple addition.

Brand Relationship Maps

The simplest way to preserve the distinction between consumers' attitudes and brand attitudes is to use a two-dimensional map to plot the two, as illustrated in Figure 2.5.

In the map, the relationship is represented as a vector, with both strength and direction. For descriptive purposes, this is the simplest approach consistent with the relational model. Conceptually, the key point that the brand relationship map reminds us of is that – unlike in an additive model – point B ("Good" Image, "Bad" Attitude) is not equivalent to point A ("Bad" Image, "Good" Attitude). In the chapters following this, brand relationship maps will be used to illustrate and analyze a number of different brand case histories – based on both qualitative and quantitative data. For more rigorous statistical purposes, such as the model described in Chapter 8, the simple brand relationship map

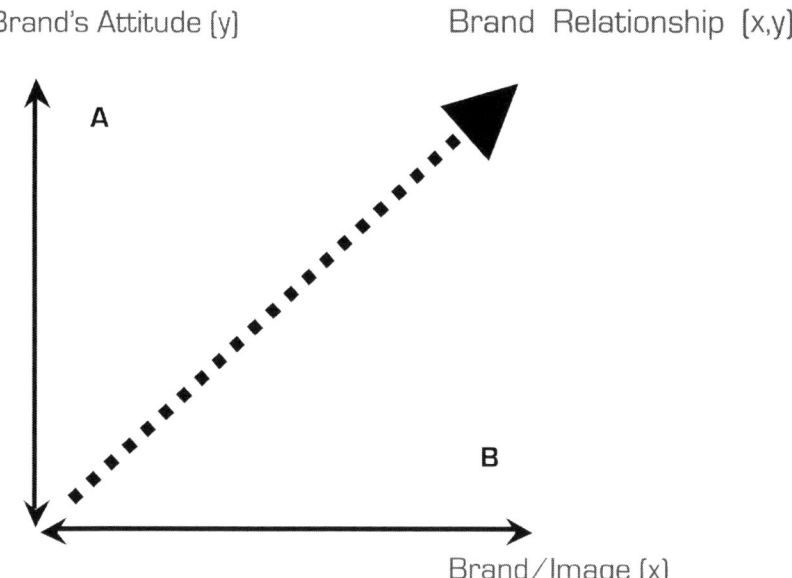

Brand's Attitude (y)

Brand Relationship (x,y)

A

B

Brand/Image (x)

FIGURE 2.5   The Brand Relationship Map

may not be sufficient; I have described in Chapter 8 a computational approach that was inspired by Catastrophe Theory.[5]

One last point that should not be lost in this new perspective is that the concept of brand personality does not have a unique role in the relationships model – it is essentially an extension of brand image, and as such forms a part of the "objective" brand. In future, the terms "brand image" and "brand personality" will generally be used interchangeably. I arrived at the concept of brands' attitudes – representing the "subjective" brand – by extrapolation from the idea of brand personality; however, brands' attitudes and brand personality are neither identical nor interchangeable. The difference between the two is the second-order intentionality of brands' attitudes, meaning that they imply that the brand is able to think something about "me," or wants to do something for or to "me." A brand that is "fun" does not necessarily have that intentionality; a brand that "takes me out of myself" does. A "Caring" brand may or may not have that intentionality; a brand that "Cares about me" or "Cares what I think" definitely does. Distinguishing between the two is central to the analysis of brand relationships.

Other Consumer Brand Relationship Models

The term Brand Relationships has become so ubiquitous that it now verges on losing any specific meaning. Unheard of 30 years ago, when I first used the term in print, it is now used to describe virtually any brand-consumer construct or interaction. With the more universal recognition that the creation of value in brands has something to do with consumers, as well as brands' owners and managers, Brand Relationships seems to have replaced Brand Equity as the preferred term at the high ground of branding practice. What does it actually mean? Or, more exactly, what do the people who use the term actually mean?

By default, Brand Relationships are assumed to mean something analogous to interpersonal relationships. Most users of the term in a specific sense – as opposed to its use as a generic surrogate for the term Brand Equity – are comfortable with the application of the interpersonal relationships (IPR) model to brands.

There are a number of variations in the specific IPR model adopted, and the methods and approaches to measurement that they employ. Several models involve no more than placing a brand on a unidimensional scale, which at its simplest goes from a bi-polar hate/love to a more articulated semantic scale, which goes from "New" to "Divorce" via "Dating," "Love," and "Boredom." Fournier, Aaker and others[6] have used more nuanced 1PR models, which have demonstrated that it is possible to use IPR-based taxa to describe various types of relationships that consumers have with a brand. That is to say, the qualities which consumers attribute to their relationship with a brand are often very similar – if not identical – to the stereotypical qualities of a specific interpersonal relationship.

However, being able to deconstruct the relationship that a specific consumer has with a specific brand, and labeling it in IPR terms, does not provide a methodology for mapping on to an IPR taxonomy the generality of consumer brand relationships. In fact, attempts to generalize and quantify the correspondence between CBR and IPR have been less than successful. When, for example, consumers are asked to allocate brands to specific IPR descriptors, their selection is highly idiosyncratic because it is specific to consumers' own personal relationships and to their own brand experiences. The idiosyncratic nature of the ways in which consumers anthropomorphize brands and their relationships with them is illustrated by the following two examples from qualitative explorations of brand relationships.

In a study of auto insurance brands in the USA, respondents' preferred brand was anthropomorphized in figures as widely different as "a benign king who knows what is best for his subjects" and "my child's pediatrician." The common underlying relational components that can be identified in these anthropomorphisms are:

- the perception of an authority figure who has knowledge and expertise that the customer lacks, combined with
- confidence that the authority figure has the best interests of the customer at heart.

The relationship with the brand is determined by the psychological inter-action of consumers' attitudes – perceptions of authority – and the projected attitudes of the brand – having the best interests of the customer at heart. The expression of that relationship anthropomorphically is highly idiosyncratic.

In a study of toilet paper conducted in Israel, a premium brand known for its strength (as opposed to the category benefit of softness) was variously described by non-users of the brand as "like Santa Claus" or a "foreign fashion model." What are the underlying elements common to both here?

- both figures are perceived as somewhat exotic (Santa in a Jewish country!) with unique competencies, but (and probably because of this perception)
- a distance, a lack of intimacy with the consumer, an indispensable element of a trusting relationship.

What each of these cases illustrate are the diverse ways in which consumers can describe what are essentially similar relationships with a brand. From the anthropomorphisms we can get to the underlying psychology of the relation-ship, using the tools of semiotics or analysis of archetypes. But we cannot go in the opposite direction – from knowing the psychology of the relationship to predicting how it will be recognized or expressed in terms of interpersonal relationships. The psychological model on which I have based my Relational Branding methodology goes directly to the heart of the Consumer Brand Relationship, rather than to its expression. In Chapter 1 we showed how brands' attitudes, as projected by the consumer, can be measured as a distinct and largely independent construct from consumers' brand perceptions. In the remainder of the book I show how these two constructs interact in a variety of different contexts.

Brand Relationships in Context

A brand's image and personality has to be appropriate for what the product is and what it does. Generally speaking, products with "serious" functions have to have the personality to go with their functions – and vice versa. The idea of a "fun" cold medication is as ridiculous as that of a clinically-tested candy bar (I am of course referring to strategic positioning – not advertising executions, in which humor may indeed be used to convey a serious message, or phony gravitas a light-hearted one). Brands' attitudes too – just like brand image – have to fit the product category. This means that certain types of brand relationships tend to be more appropriate to each product category, and that certain types of brand relationship develop because of the nature of the product category.

Sometimes the connection between the product category and the type of brand relationship is intrinsic to the product – either because of its specific function (like cold medication) or because of the level of risk that the consumer experiences in choosing the brand. Choosing a cold medication represents a potential risk to the recovery of health; spending several thousand dollars on an automobile represents a potential risk both to the buyer's future financial health as well as his self-respect. As discussed earlier in this chapter, the presence of a high level of consumer risk favors certain types of brand positioning, and therefore certain types of brand relationship. Chapter 5 is in fact devoted to exploring the reciprocal influences of risk and brand relationships.

The constraints on or catalysts for certain types of brand relationship can also arise out of extrinsic characteristics of the product category. As in many spheres, history often exerts its influence on the present. For example, consumers' relationships with many telephone companies and gas and electricity suppliers – markets that in most of Western Europe and the USA are increasingly deregulated and competitive – are ineluctably shaped by their origins as national or local monopolies. Another example is the way which, in the USA and many other countries, other brands of carbonated soft drink all have to position themselves in relation to Coca Cola; in this connection, it is interesting to see the more independent positioning of brands like Fanta (orange soda) in France and other countries where the presence of "the real thing" was historically less all-pervasive. Cultural influences, of course, often play a role in shaping the types of brand relationship that develop; different national cultures, for example, shape attitudes toward food and drink in very specific ways. The role of wine in southern European countries – as a popular beverage without any "badge" connotations – does not encourage the development of the prestige-based brand relationships which result from its more "elitist" role in Anglo-Saxon cultures.

Because of these links between product categories and brand relationships, it is much more instructive to analyze relationships within the context of product categories – or at least, types of product category – and it is this logic that provides the organizing principle of the next four chapters, in which I return from the theory to the practice of brand relationships.

Notes

1 E. Ghent (1992) Foreword. In: *Relational Perspectives in Psychoanalysis*, eds. N. J. Skolnick and S. C. Warshaw. Hillsdale, NJ: Analytic Press.
2 M. Eigen (1981) The Area of Faith in Winnicott, Lacan, and Bion, *International Journal of Psychoanalysis* 62: 413–433.
3 N. J. Chodorow (1986) Toward a Relational Individualism: The Mediation of Self Through Psychoanalysis. In: *Reconstructing Individualism: Autonomy, Individuality, and the Self in Western Thought*, eds. T. C. Heller, M. Sosna, and D. E. Wellbery. Palo Alto, CA: Stanford University Press.
4 J. Riviere (1977) The Unconscious Phantasy of an Inner World Reflected in Examples from Literature. In: *New Directions in Psychoanalysis*, ed. Melanie Klein. London: Tavistock.
5 Catastrophe Theory has been successfully used to predict how the smooth relationship between two variables – say A brand (consumers' attitude toward the brand) and

Purchase Intent – may be disrupted by a third variable – a so-called "Control" variable. This theory explains the phenomenon of the "S" curve, which we often see instead of a simpler monotonic relationship between the two original variables. It has occurred to me that brand attitudes (A consumer) may well be the control variable that mediates between A brand and Purchase Intention.

6 For example:

Susan Fournier, Consumers and Their Brands: Developing Relationship Theory in Consumer Research, *Journal of Consumer Research* 24(4) (March 1998): 343–353; Jennifer Aaker, Susan Fournier, and S. Adam Brasel, When Good Brands Do Bad, *Journal of Consumer Research* 31(1) (2004): 1–16.

3

RELATIONSHIPS WITH PACKAGED GOODS BRANDS

At first acquaintance with the brand relationships model, people often find it easier to see its application to service brands, like banks or car rental companies, or even to corporate brands. For more tangible and everyday products, such as packaged goods, the concept can seem at first difficult to relate to. What kind of attitudes can a brand of soap have? How does a frozen dinner express its feelings? The fact that these sorts of questions arise about packaged goods brands is reason enough to start my account of specific brands' relationships in these categories, but there are also a number of other reasons why – in my mind – packaged goods make the ideal starting point for exploring brands' relationships. We – both as consumers and as marketers – all know the brands in these categories very well. But the very fact of that close familiarity, and the presence of so many well-established and well-known brands, makes positioning or repositioning a packaged goods brand one of the more challenging tasks for the marketer. So the question I wish to address in this chapter is not just how the brand relationships model applies to these categories, but also how it can help in the practical task of brand building.

"Packaged goods" – or "fast moving consumer goods," as they are known in the UK – is not a product category, but it represents a group of categories – food and drink, toiletries, health and beauty aids, detergents and household cleansers – which are very significant both for the consumer and the marketing professional. For the latter, these categories are where brands made their first appearance and, consequently, are those in which branding has its longest history and greatest "depth." It is also probably the case that brands in these categories are having to play "catch-up" the most energetically, in order to adapt their marketing to digital channels. Marketing professionals who are today in their fifties or older probably cut their "marketing teeth" on packaged goods. Wherever one grew up, there are brands one remembers from childhood – of coffee, of soap, of confectionery – which still exist today. Aside from their personal significance for us, these generational brands – consciously or unconsciously – represent the models for much of our subsequent thinking about brands. For consumers, relationships with brands of packaged goods have an intensity that can be lacking in other categories. Packaged goods brands are those they transact with most frequently – purchasing, repeat purchasing, weighing the price/value balance against that of competing brands, deciding not to purchase. Relationships with brands in these categories are thus under a continual process of either renewal and reaffirmation or re-evaluation and possible rejection. In addition, most packaged goods brands serve intensely intimate functional purposes for their consumers –nourishing and refreshing them, grooming and beautifying their persons, cleaning and caring for their immediate personal environment, their clothes, and homes.

Hedonic Consumption

In order to understand the nature and role of brands' attitudes – and hence their relationships – in these categories, we have to expand the concept of what "consuming" means to the consumer. Using a brand does not just mean "solving" a functional problem – satisfying hunger or thirst, removing odor and dirt; it also usually involves experiencing a range of associative memories, emotions, and fantasies, all of which go under the heading of "hedonic" consumption. We are all familiar with the way in which particular tastes or smells can remind us of specific places we have been, particular times in our lives, or certain people we have known. The associated memory can enhance or modify the current tasting or smelling experience, making it "more" than it is – more pleasurable, more unpleasant, more intense, more significant. Hedonic consumption can also mean experiencing emotions or fantasies that are not based in any "historic" reality – or at least none that we would easily recognize. But in our inner reality – the same place that we keep our internal representations of brands – these experiences act just like memories, to enhance or modify the functional experience of using the brand. Hedonic consumption works in parallel with actual physical consumption of the product. In the consumer's internal representation, the brand triggers emotions relating to basic drives – pleasure, duty, being loved, being comforted; as a consequence – in the external world – the brand is perceived to work better, more reliably, or differently than its competitors.

The key to using this knowledge in the practical task of brand positioning is to insure that the emotions triggered by the brand – its attitudes – dovetail with and are appropriate to the functional purpose that the consumer uses it for.

Relationships with Food and Drink Brands

Food and drink products have to satisfy more different types of consumer need than probably any other type of product category. This is one of those truisms that must be experienced personally in order for one to understand its essential truth. I had the fortune to spend four years early in my career doing consumer research just for food companies in the Unilever group. Throughout this time, it was increasingly borne in on me how comprehensive and complex was the process of evaluation of a food product by the consumer. A food product has to satisfy all but one of the senses – it has to look good, smell good, feel good – mouth and hand feel – and of course taste good. (Sometimes, it has to sound good too – remember "Snap, Crackle and Pop"?) A food product usually has to satisfy nutritional or refreshment needs, and may have to measure up to certain specific situational requirements – convenience, for snacking, or just as a "displacement" activity. It must provide a minimum level of reassurance about the absence of harmful effects – and sometimes meet expectations of positive benefits in addition to the sensory, nutritional, or situational. Food products are bought for family as well as individual consumption; they therefore have significance for the consumer's role as provider/gatherer for other members of the family or social group. Brands of food products have to encapsulate and communicate all these layers of meaning just in order to satisfy consumers' functional needs. Then, to be successful, a food brand has to establish positive relationships based on the "higher" orders of meaning – objective (cultural and social) and subjective – which all successful brands have to achieve.

Relationships with Brands of Coffee – Maxwell House and Folgers

Relationships with traditional beverage brands – like tea and coffee or beer and some other alcoholic beverages – are a rich confluence of different types of meaning – cultural and social, functional, and hedonic. In North America, there is a very strong coffee tradition with broad cultural significance. How have individual coffee brands managed the process of navigating these cultural currents while also establishing their relationships with individual consumers?

At the end of the 1980s the major brands in the coffee category – after a decade of cost-cutting and so-called Trade "Marketing" – were trying to regain their leverage with the consumer. There were a number of reasons for this – first a swing of the pendulum in marketing management, with a return to the idea that higher brand value depends ultimately on high value in the consumer's eyes. Second, the major brands were also attempting to increase margins and profitability by spinning off premium variants of the mother brands; in order to use brand equity – for extending the brand – it was clear that brand equity had also to be reinforced and rebuilt. Last, although this was before the Starbucks invasion of the whole of the US, the fact that many consumers in major markets were beginning to show a preference for "gourmet" coffees over the traditional brands set off alarm signals at Kraft-General Foods (now part of Mondelez International) and Procter & Gamble – the two brand owners concerned.

Maxwell House – whose brand positioning in the 1970s had been built on a taste promise – "Good to the Last Drop" – had throughout most of the 1980s been using a variety of "Life Style" advertising campaigns. There was the feeling that – although these had promoted the social and situational values that are very central to the coffee experience – the brand had moved too far away from a taste-based positioning. Folgers, on the other hand, had fairly consistently been promoting its genuine ("Mountain Grown") coffee taste. The positioning of Maxwell House had to move back toward the taste of the coffee in order to even up the battle with Folgers. What was happening in relationship terms?

In comparing the taste of the two brands, consumers invariably rated Folgers higher on the key taste dimension of "rich." This coincided with a feeling that Folgers was delivering the expected coffee consumption experience more fully, more genuinely, less unstintingly. Maxwell House, on the other hand, was delivering just the memory of that experience. The Folgers brand (the objective brand), by its focus on the taste experience, was reinforcing consumers' subjective brand as *a source of pleasure and stimulation*, and hence enhancing the consumption experience – making it richer. Maxwell House was drawing just on the subjective brand – the memory – for that enhancement. The difference in the attitude of the two brands was that Folgers was *giving* its consumers what they remembered and what they expected; Maxwell House was *taking for granted* that its consumers would remember what they had been expecting. This particular brand attitude – giving or taking (or not giving) – is often key for food brands. We shall see it again, in a slightly different form, in the next example. It is important to point out that although it was an attitude related to an important functional attribute of the brand, it did not, in the case of Maxwell House, result from an actual inferior taste (in blind taste testing, consumers preferred both equally). It was purely a function of the brand's attitude.

Relationships with Brands of Frozen Food – Lean Cuisine

By the beginning of the 1980s diet foods had gone mainstream in the USA. Led by Coke and Pepsi, whose diet varieties provided nearly all of those brands' growth between 1980 and 1987, low or zero calorie products transitioned from being for people with a weight problem to being lifestyle products, which could be embraced by anyone. Along with this transition came a dramatic shift in consumers' expectations and requirements of diet brands – they had to taste good. Consumers of diet foods were no longer content to "punish" themselves for being overweight by eating bland calorie-less products, or by denying themselves the pleasures of the table. Low calorie was a necessary but no longer sufficient condition for success in the diet market.

Stouffer's Lean Cuisine caught and held the crest of this wave throughout most of the decade. A very successful extension of Stouffer's mainstream "Red Box" range of frozen dinners and frozen entrees, Lean Cuisine started out with the benefits of the Stouffer's image for quality and taste, and quickly established its own independent brand equity based on an image of really good tasting products which happened also to be low calorie – "all this for less than 300 calories." Lean Cuisine developed a very wide range of upscale-image products, with Italian, French, and Mexican style sub ranges featured in its advertising. In actual fact, the bulk of its sales were of traditional products like spaghetti meat balls and ravioli cheese – the products that Americans like to eat – but such mainstream products never besmirched the brand's advertising, which was graced only with entrees of the class of Chicken Cacciatore and Lasagna Verde. Midway through the decade, Lean Cuisine was comfortably leading competitors such as Weight Watchers (which, despite energetic attempts to refurbish its rather dowdy image, suffered from the heritage of its name and denial-oriented origins) and the diet sub-brands of other mainstream frozen food brands.

In 1990, the name of the game changed once more. ConAgra, a large food conglomerate, launched a range of products – including frozen entrees – under the Healthy Choice brand name. The Healthy Choice platform was very straightforward – no longer were low calories sufficient to insure healthy eating; the product had to be low sodium and low fat as well. The pitch was made in their advertising by the ConAgra CEO who related how, since his heart attack, he had been eating in a new way, which was recommended for everyone who wanted to stay healthy and avoid heart disease. The impact was immediate and quite dramatic. Lean Cuisine was completely "wrong-footed" and started to lose share to Healthy Choice (which turned out to be the most successful new food brand entry in a decade). It was at this point that Lean Cuisine started to review its brand strategy; included as part of that review was a brand relationships analysis, based on qualitative research among consumers of the three major brands of diet frozen entree.[1]

All consumers – irrespective of whether they used Lean Cuisine or not – had a very similar image of the objective brand and its personality. The "persona" of the brand that emerged was that of an attractive woman in her thirties. Associated with affluence and success, Lean Cuisine always looked extremely elegant and stylish, and never "dressed casually." The brand personality of Lean Cuisine was described as very active, energetic, and ambitious – "she takes good care of herself." The objective Lean Cuisine brand was very clear and consistent, and perfectly in line with the image of the products; Lean Cuisine epitomized taste – both literally and figuratively. It is only when we moved on to the brand's attitudes that we found a divergence of opinion – on the issue of how *generous* Lean Cuisine was.

Only the very loyal users of the brand perceived Lean Cuisine as a generous person, who shared her gifts with others. In contrast, non-users saw the brand as totally selfish, self-centered, and not caring at all about them. Occasional users − the largest segment of the brand's consumers − saw Lean Cuisine as rather self-absorbed − inward looking, if not totally self-centered.

We went through this same process for Lean Cuisine's competitors − Healthy Choice and Weight Watchers − and were able to map out the relationships between consumers and all three brands, as shown in Figure 3.1.

On the horizontal dimension, representing brand personality, Lean Cuisine occupies one extreme, Weight Watchers the opposite, and Healthy Choice lies between the two. Lean Cuisine, as we have seen, is ambitious, achievement-oriented, independent, hard-working, elegant, and stylish. At the other end, Weight Watchers was described as passive, dependent, slow-paced, and not goal-oriented. Healthy Choice occupies an intermediate position, closer to Lean Cuisine than to Weight Watchers, but with several important differences − more down to earth, more straightforward, more casual, and simpler.

The vertical dimension defines the attitudes of the brands − varying from *selfish to generous*. As we have already seen, Lean Cuisine's attitudes vary across the full length of the spectrum depending on whether people were users of the brand and, if so, how loyal they were to it. In contrast, both Healthy Choice and Weight Watchers were generally seen as having generous attitudes.

Lean Cuisine's loss of share was the result of its losing many of its occasional users to Healthy Choice. At first glance, the problem seemed to be

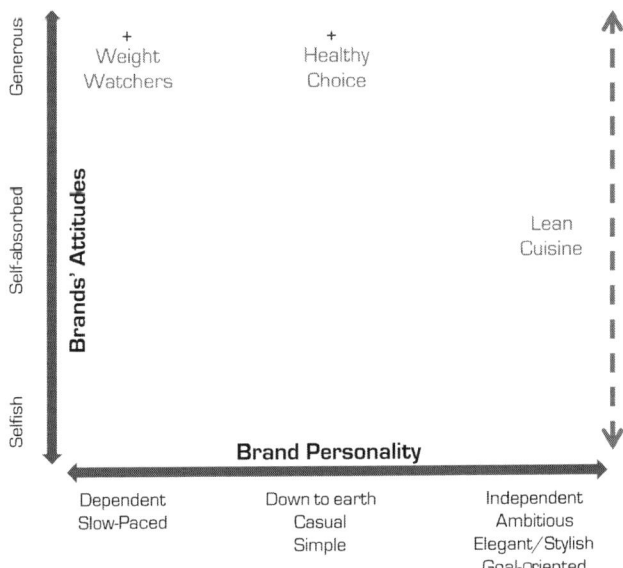

FIGURE 3.1 Diet Frozen Entrees Brand Relationship Map

Lean Cuisine's personality – too upscale, too much of an achiever. It was tempting to conclude that the brand personality should be pushed more into the mainstream of middle America, and that the advertising should show middle Americans eating middle American meals (like spaghetti meat balls and maccaroni cheese). But Lean Cuisine's stylish, independent, ambitious personality in fact represented its "edge" over Healthy Choice – greater "style" in the brand personality went hand-in-hand with a perceived taste advantage. *This brand personality only became negative when it was accompanied by a more selfish attitude.* Trying to make Lean Cuisine more mainstream would inevitably move it closer to the brand personality of Healthy Choice – more down to earth, casual, and simple. This would have risked the dissipation of the brand's key equities, as its positioning became merely a "me too" of Healthy Choice.

The conclusion of the analysis of Lean Cuisine's relationships was to focus on developing a more "generous" attitude for the brand – not to try and make it more "down to earth," like Healthy Choice. The advertising for Lean Cuisine had always been rather "narcissistic," showing just beautiful young women and admiring men – but never their families. We felt that the Lean Cuisine "style" could easily be retained, while showing the brand in a more "sharing" mode. The Lean Cuisine personality would be much more accessible if it was seen to be combined with a generous attitude. This by itself would not, of course, answer the challenge posed by Healthy Choice, but it would allow Lean Cuisine to maintain and strengthen its brand equity while it adjusted its products to the new requirements of the marketplace. Lean Cuisine would continue to be the brand of really good tasting products, which happened also to be healthy – in the new expanded sense.

The Lean Cuisine case is a prime example of a masterfully crafted brand image marred by a totally unmanaged brand's attitude. It illustrates a number of important advantages of the relationship approach to brand positioning. First, that emphasis on the separate identification of the two dimensions of the brand relationship gives a much clearer picture of both the strengths and weaknesses of the brand. If this clear distinction had not been made, there was a real danger that Lean Cuisine would have been completely repositioned – which would have "thrown out the baby with the bath water." Second, the fact that brands' attitudes – representing the subjective brand – can be crafted just as readily as brand image and brand personality provides a whole new set of dimensions of "positioning space" – even in crowded packaged goods categories – and a new set of tools for marketing management.

In the brand relationships of both Maxwell House and Lean Cuisine, generosity, (and its opposite) was the key brand attitude – the Achilles Heel of both brands. This attitude is fundamental to many food brands, because of the role of food as nourishment. As well as satisfying the palate and the stomach, a food brand has to trigger the emotion of feeling nourished. There are a number of ways that food brands can fall short on this dimension; they can, like Lean Cuisine, focus single-mindedly – and successfully – on one aspect of the brand's image, while neglecting to manage the brand's attitudes. In fact, the more distinctive is the image of a brand, the more assiduously its attitudes have to be managed – we shall see that again in the next chapter in relation to the American Express brand. Alternatively, like Maxwell House, a brand can seem to want to give less to its consumers if it loses its focus on a central category benefit. Sometimes it can be perceptions of pack or portion size that create an impression of a lack of open-handed attitude toward the consumer, and sometimes a failure to manage perceptions of value.

Relationships with Brands of Health and Beauty Aids

The available positionings for a brand in one of the HBA categories are all variations of one of the following:

- rational/functional
- authority
- pleasure.

Both rational and authoritative positionings emphasize the end-benefits to the consumer. Both require a "permission to believe," based on either product ingredients or brand heritage – or both. In contrast, a positioning based on pleasure focuses on the process of using the product, rather than the promised end-benefits. If a brand promises end-benefits, then there must be a credible rationale linking either the image of the brand or the product ingredients – or both – to the end-benefits. With a pleasure-based positioning, the image of the brand and the product ingredients *are* the end-benefit. Thus, most brands of deodorant or toothpaste stress the ingredients that make the product more efficacious, whereas many shower and bath products concentrate on the sensory aspects of the product – its fragrance, the lather, the feel of the product in-use. These categories represent extremes of the end-benefit (effectiveness) versus in-use (enjoyment) positioning spectrum, in which the nature of the categories themselves tends to define and limit the possibilities for brand positioning; what are more interesting are categories in which both types of positioning are viable.

Hair care is a category in which there are a multitude of brands in each market, yet the same five or six international brands – and the same two or three multinational brand owners – dominate in each. The "high ground" positioning is an authoritative claim for better end results – more shiny, beautiful-looking hair, healthier hair and scalp, more manageable hair. The high ground also, of course, commands a premium. While many people just wash their hair, there are indeed others for whom the appearance and health of their hair represents a daily concern. The latter are looking for a particular type of support from their hair care brand, which is best catered for by an authoritative brand positioning. For a hair care brand to take an authoritative positioning it must have a very credible platform such as the "science" of Procter & Gamble's Pantene, which has a global brand share of over 7 percent, or "professionalism" like the salon credentials of Vidal Sassoon (also P&G). The point to remember, however, is that the consumer is able to judge the results of using the brand. The greater the authority that the brand evokes, the higher will be the expectations for the desired end-benefits. So in this category, an authoritative positioning has to deliver (we will see in Chapter 5 how, in other categories, the consumer may be prepared to give the authoritative brand the "benefit of the doubt"). But even so, just as in food, the hedonic factor in consumption means that the appropriate brand attitude can enhance and modify the consumer's perception of the end results – and also help justify paying a premium price. Usually, the brand needs to adopt some form of the "taking responsibility" attitude, described in Chapter 2.

Not all hair care brands can, however, deliver the results required by an authoritative positioning. The stakes are high, and very few brand owners have the resources to insure that their brand can keep up. For these brands, rather than competing as also-rans in the high-performance race, a pleasure positioning may be much more effective. A pleasure positioning does not set up high expectations about end results; it requires only that consumers should *enjoy using the brand*. Not only does the consumer not expect too much from the brand, but the brand does not "expect" the consumer to live up to it. In this sense, use of the brand is more free of "risks" – the risk of results not living up to expectations, the risk of having made the wrong choice. It is the ideal positioning for a non-premium priced hair care brand. A pleasure positioning, too, must be accompanied by the appropriate brand attitude. These alternative brand relationships are also present in another HBA category, bar soaps.

Consumers' Relationships with Dove and Other Brands of Soap

Although Dove is one of the greatest and oldest of packaged goods brands, it has only recently – in the last 20 years or so – burst out from its North American origins to take the world by storm. The original bar soap has now been successfully extended into liquid soap and a variety of skin and hair care products, all of which share in – and contribute to – the brand's enviable equity. This case history, however, concerns the original Dove soap, and dates from 1989 – before the brand's global expansion.

Dove's positioning is based on a strong end-benefit – "will not dry your face like soap" – supported by a very clear ingredient claim – "contains one quarter moisturizing cream." The image of the moisturizing cream pouring into the bar – the so-called "pour shot" – was mandated by David Ogilvy, who originally created Dove's advertising in 1955, and still appears in every advertisement for the brand. At the time of this brand relationships analysis, Dove users were typically women aged 30 and over, who were not concerned about using bar soap on their face. They appreciated the soft feel of their skin after washing with Dove, and also noted the effects – soft and smooth looking – on the appearance of their skin. Although Dove had, of course, never made any claim about keeping skin younger – and few users would ever have openly admitted to that expectation – this fantasy undoubtedly underlay the loyalty of many of the brand's users, and their willingness to pay a premium for it in a category which was notorious for aggressive price promoting.

Dove had a solid core of loyal users and also a much wider group of women who used it regularly but not exclusively. The objective of the brand relationship analysis was to explore ways in which the loyal segment could be expanded; it was based on consumer research among three segments – women who used Dove as their main brand, those who used it occasionally but were not loyal to it, and those who did not use Dove at all.

Relationships with Dove covered the full spectrum of positioning opportunities for HBA brands.

- For some women, their relationship with Dove was purely functional – they appreciated it for its gentle, non-drying characteristics and liked it for moisturizing their skin. If there was any hedonic element to their use of Dove, it was insufficient to create a stronger bond with the brand than with any other, and would certainly not justify their paying a premium for it.
- The majority of Dove's loyal users saw Dove in a "Caring" relationship toward them. The consumer's internal representation of Dove took responsibility – in a loving and nurturing fashion – for the welfare of her complexion. The objective brand was a gentle authority (moisturizer ingredient) that cared *for* her skin by not drying it out and by keeping it feeling soft. The subjective Dove cared *about* her skin, and wanted it to feel and look younger. Dove's caring attitude – not its moisturizer – gave the user permission to believe that the benefits of using the brand would go beyond the immediate ones of being gentle and non-drying.
- There was, in addition, a sizeable group – consisting of both loyal and occasional users – for whom the essence of their relationship with Dove was the experience of using it. They took pleasure in its soft and creamy feel on their skin, and the quality of its abundant lather. The brand's personality – like the product itself – was gentle, uncomplicated, and even childlike. Because they did not expect too much from Dove– it did not have to produce lasting effects for their skin – Dove did not have expectations of them – in contrast to the caring relationship, *it did not expect them to be concerned about their skin*. Dove did not have responsibilities, and therefore encouraged them to feel similarly free of responsibility. The physical characteristics of the brand allowed them to indulge and pamper themselves; the open, non-judgmental attitude toward them allowed them to feel emotionally "liberated," and hence made the experience of using Dove even more pleasurable.

Among its regular users, Dove's "Caring" relationship dominated the other two. It was the brand's attitude of "caring *about*" that played the crucial role in this relationship; it allowed loyal users to believe in an end result – keeping them looking younger – that the brand could never have explicitly claimed.

Although many occasional or infrequent users also liked Dove and felt positive toward it, the brand generally had either a functional or an experiential relationship with them. Dove is essentially a face soap – which means that that is how people think of it, but not necessarily how they use it. People buy Dove with facial use in mind, but once it is in their bathrooms it is also likely to be used as a general bath and shower soap. As such, its good lathering properties are appreciated, and contribute toward a pleasurable use experience. This is how the brand has established an experiential relationship with some regular and many occasional users. Although this relationship is undoubtedly positive, it lacks the unique strength of the "caring" relationship. Objectively speaking, Dove lacks two key functional characteristics for this type of relationship – a deodorant ingredient and fragrance (Dove does have varieties with fragrance, but the "canonical" Dove, the Dove that established its relationships with many of its consumers, is fragrance-free). Gentleness – an essential aspect of Dove's brand personality – is not typical of the brand personality of the deodorant bath and shower soap, which tends to be brasher, more assertive, and showy.

Over in this part of the bar soap world, there is another cast of characters – like Zest, Lever 2000, Irish Spring, and Coast – which either have very extrovert "bubbly" personalities to go with their existential perfume and bubbly lather, or which project the "aspirational" lifestyles of their users. These brands all have the function of removing body odor and replacing it with their own. The lather (odor removal) and the fragrance (odor replacement) are the evidence of their functionality, which is why the essence of these brands' relationships is in the experience. The consumer's relationship with the brand is either consummated in the shower – or not at all. Aside from getting clean, what users want from this experience is a renewal of "me-ness," a reaffirmation of their own familiar identity. It is not surprising, therefore, that the brand they want to share the experience with should be like them, with an attitude that validates and reinforces their own feeling of identity.

Relationships with Fabric Softener Brands

My last case in packaged goods categories takes us into the area of fabric washing products – sometimes thought of as purely "functional" categories. By that designation, people generally mean that brands of washing powders and detergents are all evaluated objectively by the consumer on the basis of what they do – or claim to do – for the wash. The totality of positioning in this category was often regarded – usually by people from outside of it – as a question of whitening power versus safety for colors, efficient stain removal as against being kind to fabrics, etc. The opportunity for any emotional life for these brands was seen as minimal. It is also true that much of the advertising in this category until fairly recently conspired to support this perception. Advertising was all "about" the product and the results it would achieve; with few exceptions – the most notable early exception being probably the Persil "Mum" in the UK – there was little deliberate effort to inject these brands' communications with any emotional values.

Fabric softeners were perhaps the first breach in the dam. Although the product had an unambiguous function – softening fabrics, masking residual detergent smells with a more pleasant fragrance, and restoring some of the "fluffiness" of the fibers – it also provided – or perhaps restored – an emotional benefit to the user; "involvement" in the washing process. Fabric softener brands were intended to offer the user – by that time virtually just a bystander to the inexorable escalation of washing machine and fabric detergent technologies – the opportunity for intervention and participation in the process. A fabric softener allowed the user to affect the end result of the wash, to give it a feminine touch of softness and sweet fragrance.

There is no doubt that this thinking was correct; by 2014, US sales of fabric softeners were in excess of 6 billion dollars. The detergents companies had done their research well, and had identified a real need. However – despite this – there was a sense in which use of this product was felt to be superfluous to the real function of washing clothes; after all, clothes had been successfully cleaned before fabric softeners were invented, so how could the use of an additional product – at an additional cost – be now justified? The cost, of course, was a real issue, and was often represented as the reason for not using the product. But the barrier was not just the actual price that had to be paid for the product – there was a psychological price too. That price was the guilt that many consumers felt about "indulging" themselves with an additional product which was not strictly "necessary." The fact was that it was just as necessary as any other product that meets an unsatisfied need; but in this case, the functional need was often seen as ephemeral, leaving the emotional need too uncomfortably exposed for many consumers.

The detergents companies responded in different ways to the challenge of making the product category more acceptable. P&G was first into the product category with its Downy brand (Lenor in Europe), and generally enjoyed – as it still does – the benefits of first arrival. In true P&G fashion, it sought to give the product an ever more convincing and impressive functionality, in the effort to "legitimize" its use. Demonstrations of towering piles of towels mightily fluffed-up by Downy/Lenor were the order of the day, amply supported by a variety of ingredients claims. Ironically, therefore, Downy/Lenor followed the hallowed tradition of earlier fabrics washing products in emphasizing performance and product technology, rather than the emotional benefits that the product category had initially promised. But Downy/Lenor was successful, because it effectively set a new standard for laundry results; softness, fluffiness, and pleasant fragrance soon all became normal expectations, rather than optional extras. In brand relationship terms, Downy/Lenor successfully occupied an authoritative positioning in most markets, by guaranteeing – taking over responsibility for – the end results of the wash (once again leaving the housewife on the sidelines). Thanks to its positioning and to the premium price it commands in most markets, Downy/Lenor is a comfortable brand leader in terms of value shares in many markets.

Unilever, after some attempts to play catch-up in the performance stakes, opted for an altogether different brand relationship strategy – equivalent to the experiential relationships in the toiletries categories that I described earlier in this chapter. The Unilever companies in Europe and North America, one after another, launched a new brand of fabric softener, *at a substantially lower price than Downy/Lenor*, whose brand symbol was a cuddly toy bear which became the "spokesthing" for the brand – on the package and in the advertising, bouncing around in the laundry, while proclaiming its softness in its sweet little voice. This brand and the relationships it aspired to with consumers was truly "engineered" from the outset; Unilever even eschewed its normal international brand naming policy in favor of a series of different national brand names, all of which were "meaningful" in their respective languages – Snuggle in the USA, Coccolino in Italy, Cajoline in France, Kuschelweich in Germany, Mimosin in Spain – and all of which supported the soft cuddly personality of the brand.

Virtually everywhere, the new brand exceeded expectations in terms of the marketing results that were achieved (in some countries, cautious managers were reluctant to believe the results of their own test markets and research-based projections). The brand's attitude worked purely and simply on the pleasure principle – "enjoy." Snuggle and its European avatars invited consumers to come and "play," to put their *own* mark on the laundry process; and if that mark was less evident in the final result, it did not matter because the benefit was paid off *during* the process. The brand emphasized the user's role, rather than asserting its own; it respected and validated users' real needs, rather than defining new ones.

Part of the brand's success was undoubtedly due to its lower price; but a lower price by itself would not have worked. Not only did it lower the monetary price for using it, the brand's attitude lowered the psychological price as well. Although Downy/Lenors' super-performance was evidently attractive, it left many consumers in the same place they had always been. For as many who aspired to the new performance standards set by Downy/Lenor there were probably an equal number who found these to be demotivating, and who were even intimidated by the idea of having to achieve demonstrably better results from the laundry in order to justify the additional cost of the product. Engineering Snuggle's attitude into the brand from the outset was a superb example of relational brand positioning.

Onwards and Upwards?

In this chapter, we have seen how the phenomenon of hedonic consumption – emotions triggered by tastes, smells, or any other brand cues, which can either strengthen or weaken brand relationships – is such an important element in packaged goods categories. It provides the link between the functionality of the product and the brand relationship, a channel for the reciprocal exchange of influences. It is because of this phenomenon that brand relationships in these categories can be thought of as arising out of the product itself and its specific functionality. In the next chapter, I move on to a type of product category – prestige brands – in which, for the most part, brand relationships are extrinsic to the product. The influences on and by brand relationships in these categories are cultural and social; but this different dynamic does not alter the basic chemistry of the brand relationship, as the interaction of consumers' attitudes with those of the brand.

Note

1 The research methodology consisted of 30 in-depth interviews – one-on-one interviews lasting up to one hour and a half each – in which respondents were asked to imagine Lean Cuisine as a person, and to describe that person in great detail. The special interview protocol which has been developed for brand relationships research, together with a more detailed description of the research methodology, can be found in the appendix.

4

RELATIONSHIPS WITH PRESTIGE BRANDS

What is Prestige?

"Prestige" is a descriptor of a brand that implies that purchase and/or use of such a brand confers on the user some benefits over and above the basic functionality of the product. Although generally we assume that the major benefit of purchasing and/or using a prestige brand is the acquisition of higher status, there is also another type of benefit that we might term self-indulgence. Status is a measure of self, relative to other people, so it is "outer-directed"; self-indulgence deals purely with internal states; it is a form of the hedonic consumption that we met in Chapter 3; it is "inner-directed." Although prestige, the image of the brand, is a common element that they share, these are clearly different brand relationships; and if they share the same or a similar brand image – then logically, the brands' attitudes must be different.

Status vs Self-Indulgence

For the use or purchase of a brand to enhance the status of its user, the act of consumption has to be in some way public. When someone wears expensive "designer" clothing, or drives a luxury car, then the assumption is that other people will reasonably deduce that this person can afford to buy such expensive items, and their status level – in terms of perceived disposable income or spending power – will accordingly be enhanced. Status is, of course, broader than just income or wealth. I once had a boss who told me: "If you want to be significant, you must act significantly." There are many situations in which conspicuous consumption is an effective means of "acting significantly." It is, in fact, one of the oldest of humanity's cultural universals, evident not just in the use of prestige brands, but also observable in personal adornment, hospitality, and gift-giving throughout the ages and across many different cultures. As with the large and beautiful tail of the male peacock – a non-functional appendage that evolved as a result of the "arms race" between female peacocks' preference for large and beautiful tails and males' competition to attract females – it is not hard to conceptualize the Darwinian process that might have embedded this kind of showy behavior in our genes. Higher status may be an end in and of itself, or it may serve more tangible objectives – getting a better mate, a better job, or a better deal.

In contrast to the outer-directed relationship with prestige brands, which is about acquiring status, we can describe the relationship as self-indulgence when a prestige brand is used to "impress" the user himself, or herself. The benefits are all internalized; the brand speaks directly *to* the user, rather than *about* the user, and the brand relationship is different.

In practice, these two types of brand relationship are not mutually exclusive; the user can both nourish the "inner self" as well as gain status benefits by the purchase and/or use of a prestige brand; it is a question of balance. When two different brand relationships coexist, it is important to be clear on how they are both created and sustained; what elements of the brand's image are relevant for each relationship, and what brands' attitudes combine with them to create the different relationships.

Types of Brand Prestige

There are three broad routes via which brands acquire prestige, each of which has a different balance between the intangible qualities of the brand and its functionality:

- with outstanding quality and performance
- by venerability
- borrowed prestige.

The way that many brands acquire prestige is via their reputation for exceptional quality or outstanding performance qualities. Luxury or high-performance car marques, like Rolls-Royce, Mercedes, or Maserati are the most obvious examples, but many categories have their luxury brands – expensive perfumes which are made with difficult to obtain natural ingredients, high-end consumer electronics products with sophisticated components and circuitry, designer boutiques which only use precious fabrics and materials. The *raison d'être* of the Hammacher Schlemmer mail-order, and now online, catalogue is to search out and offer "the best quality" example of everything, from garden gnomes to shaving mirrors.

Brands can also acquire prestige by being venerable – pioneers which set the de facto standards for the category, by which other later entries are judged. Via this mechanism, brands can establish relationships that depend on perceptions of authority; but being old can too easily become being old and out of touch if the brand's attitude is not appropriate; apart from very traditional categories, in which technical progress and trends have little meaning, this can be a more evanescent form of prestige. In Israel, a country that saw a particularly fast growth in the penetration of cellular phones, the sole operator for the first five years was a joint venture between Motorola and the local PTT. Because of the high cost of equipment and airtime, penetration remained at less than 7 percent, and mobile telephony was seen as the perk of the business executive or the idle rich. When a second operator was franchised, with a mandate to offer very low-cost service, penetration quadrupled within two years. However, the original operator was still seen as the prestige brand, and continued to enjoy the patronage of business customers long after any real differences in service quality had ceased to exist. Then, a third franchise operated by the French group Orange entered the market, with a service based on the newer GSM technology. Virtually overnight, the banner of prestige passed from the Motorola brand to the brand with the latest technology. In the end, greater functionality trumped venerability.

Borrowed prestige, the third type, may or may not have anything to do with the functionality of the brand – past or present. It is a prestige that derives from the association of the brand with prestigious people. This, too, has its roots in history, when suppliers of various goods and services competed for the patronage of royal courts and aristocratic households. The pay-off was that the products and services of the court suppliers and craftsmen acquired a cachet that others – perhaps equally good or even better – did not enjoy. In England today, many brands still jealously guard their "royal warrant" as suppliers to HM the Queen. The plebeian version of the royal warrant comes in two varieties; one is the attachment to the brand of a prestigious designer name, which is of course no more than a borrowing of prestige previously acquired by one of the three routes. The second is the celebrity endorsement, with its implied assertion that if the brand is used by the great and glorious then some of whatever it is that they have got will rub off on the non-celebrity brand user. This is the type of prestige associated with the American Express Card, which is my first brand relationships case in this chapter.

The American Express Card

I used the example of this brand in Chapter 1 to introduce the concept of brands' attitudes, and to make the general point that an unmanaged attitude could act to the detriment of a carefully honed brand image. Here, I want to re-examine the brand more closely, specifically from the point of view of prestige.

I described in Chapter 1 how the "Do You Know Me?" advertising campaign successfully built the prestige of the brand by associating it with a variety of well-known people, representing a wide range of the domains of modern-day status. The tag line at the end of each of the advertisements in this campaign was the phrase that appears on the American Express Card itself: "Member since . . ." No other card implies that its holder is a member of anything, and it was this – almost overlooked – difference that inspired the follow-on campaign to "Do You Know Me?" in the mid 1980s, which tried to leverage and give substance to the idea of membership.

This new campaign – called "Membership Has its Privileges" – showed a variety of "power" scenarios, in which American Express Card members were able to exercise extraordinary control over their environment – leave for unexpected long-distance trips at a moment's notice, have urgently needed medications delivered to them in faraway places, get a lost card replaced in twenty-four hours anywhere in the world – all thanks to their "membership" with the American Express Card.

The American Express Card had originally been a charge card intended for an elite target. But the emergence and explosive growth of credit card brands in the mass market had shown that in order for the Amex Corporation to achieve further growth and increased shareholder value, the American Express Card needed to break out of that original positioning and try to embrace the mass market. From its origins with the Green Card, a whole stratified brand architecture had evolved; since 1966 there had been a Gold Card, and in 1984 an even more exclusive Platinum Card was launched; in an inversion of conventional color associations, the Black Card was introduced in 1999 as the most elite card. This architecture was completed at the bottom end, when the Green Card started to offer revolving credit – a big departure for American Express – in order to make it more appealing to users of regular credit cards like Visa and MasterCard.

The Green Card was now the mass market vehicle of the American Express brand. However, it met with strong resistance from many potential consumers who had the lifestyles, incomes, and creditworthiness to qualify them as American Express Green Card members. In fact, the stronger the brand's relationship became with its members, the more obdurate was the resistance to becoming one among about 50 percent of the brand's potential target. Why could the American Express Card brand not establish the same brand relationship with these prospects as it had with its members? Although the Green Card was now targeted at the mass market, it remained the icon of the American Express brand; it carried all the values – brand image and brand attitudes – accumulated over two decades of "Do You Know Me?" and "Membership Has its Privileges." Were those values now inappropriate to its new mass market mission?

Brand Image was not the problem; research studies showed that both card members and non-members gave identical ratings on key attributes, and that both groups aspired equally to these desirable qualities of a prestige brand. What consumers thought of the brand was clear and consensual. The key to the problem emerged when we asked members and non-members to tell us what the

American Express Card thought of them. Here is how many card members perceived the brand's attitude toward them:

> I know that you're a sound and creditworthy person. So, when you're with me, everyone will accept you, and treat you as an important person. Of course, it's me they really know and respect, so stick with me and you'll be OK.

The American Express Card gives the member approval, an approval that recognizes the worthiness of the card member to share in the prestige, authority, and power of the American Express Card. Other people give card members approval, because the card approves of them. The card functions as the classic status symbol; evidence of his own worth – to the member himself as well as to other people.

Now contrast that with the perceived attitude of the brand toward many non-members.

> I don't think you're my type. First of all, I'm not sure you can afford to keep up with me. Then, I'm usually in the company of well-known and important people. Does that describe you?

Whereas members felt their own worth and status to be enhanced by their association with the card, this group feels put down and intimidated by it. Even if they admire the American Express Card and aspire to acquire its prestige, there is no way that these non-members feel that they could approach it. They reject the card because they feel that the card rejects them.

So, although the same *images* were getting through to both groups, they perceived the brand's *attitude* very differently. For both groups the idea of membership successfully communicated a form of exclusivity. But to one group, it said it in a way that implied "you can belong," while to the other it said "not for you." The Brand Relationship was drastically different.

Once the problem was so clearly identified, it was not difficult to pay as much attention to managing the brand's attitudes as had previously been given just to its image and personality. For example, it was possible to balance in the advertising the portrayal of heavy-duty business-oriented lifestyles – which many non-members not only didn't identify with, but actually found intimidating – with a more reward-related and fun/relaxation context for the American Express Card. We started seeing well-heeled holidaymakers extending their vacations in order to have more fun, and radiantly pregnant mums on pre-natal shopping sprees. The message was the same; that American Express is a card for financially responsible people, which allows you to buy what you want, wherever you want to be, without any preset spending limit. But what these ads were designed to communicate was that even if your lifestyle does not include unscheduled business trips to Bangkok, American Express is still interested in you.

In Chapter 1, Figure 1.3 shows the relationship between a Prestigious brand image and an Unapproachable brands' attitude; the point was made there that it is possible to be prestigious without necessarily being unapproachable too. So how did this work out for American Express? Was that brand able to break the equation between the two? Twenty years on, the effects of the change in the brand's attitude, reflected in advertising for American Express,[1] can be seen in the measured positions of the major credit card brands in Figure 4.1.

While Discover, MasterCard, and especially Visa have all become relatively more prestigious – and more unapproachable – American Express has substantially diminished its unapproachable attitude without losing an iota of prestige.

Prestige brands, like American Express, have to build and maintain a prestige image, but that entails treading a tightrope. In order to maintain the values that make these brands aspirational, they have to keep hitting the appropriate buttons – a brand for successful or significant people, a brand for those who don't really *need* anything, a brand that will earn you respect and admiration, etc. In doing so, they risk adopting attitudes which can intimidate or alienate the potential user. This is evidently true for "everyday" prestige brands, like American Express; but the question is whether it is also true at the top end of the prestige spectrum – where prestige perhaps morphs into something else, which I will call luxury. Does the luxury brand also need to balance its ultra-prestigious image with an inclusive attitude? The answer to this question depends on whether there is a real difference between "luxury" and "prestige" in a brand, or whether luxury is just another way of describing very high prestige? Because, if that is the case, then luxury brands should play by the "rules" of any other prestige brand.

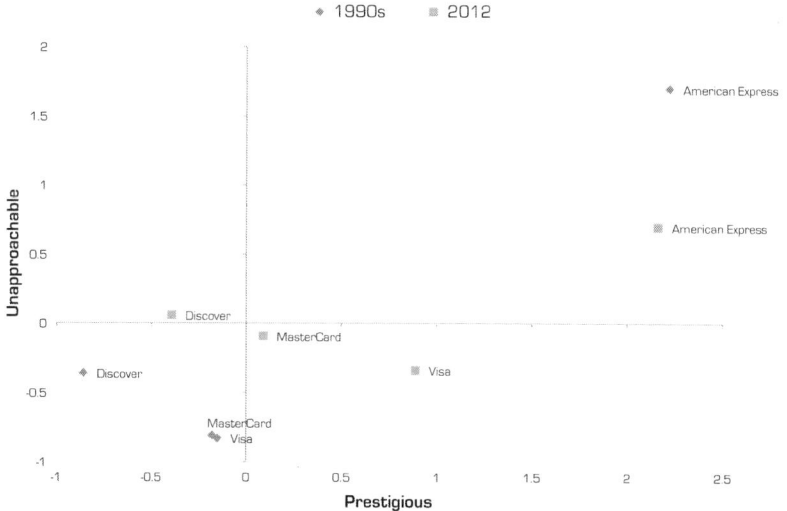

FIGURE 4.1 Credit Card Brand Relationship Map

Clearly, luxury is in the eye of the beholder, but let us suppose that there is a difference in kind as well as degree; let us define luxury as going "above and beyond." Luxury brands, let us say, exceed any possible need to such an extent that the additional functionality and values they possess are effectively redundant; more than added value, they possess "excess" value. If having excess value – qualities that everyone might want but that no one actually needs – defines the image of a luxury brand, what distinguishes the luxury brand's attitudes? Intuitively, it seems that a bit of arrogance or unapproachability in the attitude of a luxury brand may be – if not appropriate – at least harmless. Luxury brands are not for everyone; they are for an elite group; and the elite target for a luxury brand presumably has the confidence or sangfroid not to be put off by a little brand arrogance.

My hypothesis was that prestige is not a continuum, that the excess value of luxury brands and the added value of prestige brands are not just two points on the same spectrum; that there is a discontinuity between them. In the second case history of this chapter, I will illustrate that discontinuity empirically and show that while it may not always be easy to identify the point where a brand crosses the line from prestige to luxury – or vice versa – there is a clear difference, in kind as well as degree, between prestige brands' and luxury brands' attitudes.

Luxury Brands

A recent study of 20 prestige and luxury brands – designer brands, accessories, luxury retailers, and liquor brands – focused narrowly on the issue of "ultra" prestige image and the corresponding brands' attitudes. One of the ways in which consumers frequently describe the unapproachable attitude of these kinds of brands is in the phrase "Makes me feel that I'm not good enough." Figure 4.2 shows the Brand Relationship Map resulting from that specific brand's attitude and prestige image.

Here, it is difficult to argue the case – as I did in Chapter 1 – that brands can be both prestigious and have an approachable attitude. Virtually all of the brands with the highest levels of prestige (above the average of the 20 brands in the study) also have the most unapproachable attitude; while the brands with lower prestige also have a below average unapproachable brand attitude. Within these two groups too – the above and below average prestige brands – there is a very marked relationship between greater prestige and making people feel they are not good enough.

If the level of prestige that these brands possess comes with such – apparently negative – attitudinal baggage, why do people want it? Because want it they do, as the next chart shows. Figure 4.3 plots the level of prestige of each brand against the percentage saying that the brand is preferred over others.

This shows two distinct trends; the group of above average prestige brands – as a group – are substantially less likely to be described as preferred brands than the group of below average prestige brands. As I suggested earlier, there is a

FIGURE 4.2 Prestige Brands' Brand Relationship Map

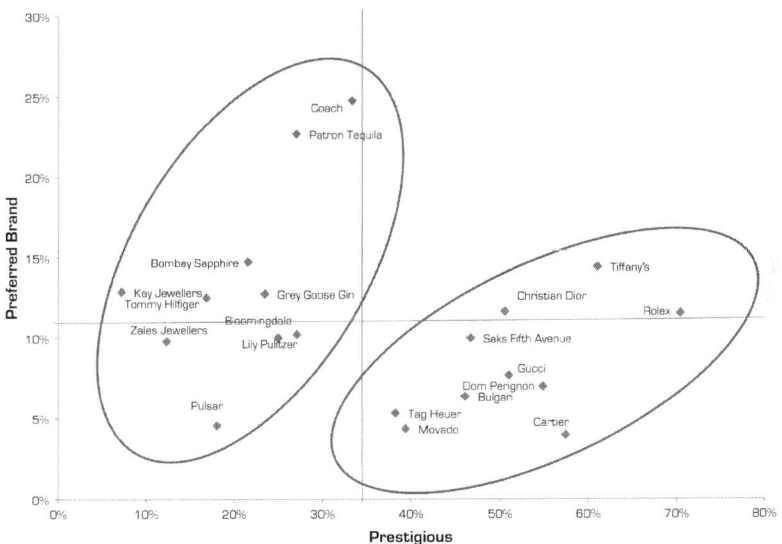

FIGURE 4.3 Prestige Brands – Preference and Brand Image

discontinuity of prestige between these two sets of brands – a difference in the kind as well as in the level of prestige – and we cannot view them as a homogeneous group. For the sake of argument, I am going to refer to the below average prestige group as "prestige" brands, and the above average prestige group as "luxury." It is important to note that *within* each of these two groups of brands, the relationship between prestige and preference is still a strongly positive one.

From Figure 4.2 we saw that for both groups – prestige and luxury brands – higher prestige is associated with a more unapproachable attitude. Perhaps, now that we have achieved a finer focus by having separated the two groups, we will find *within* each that desirable balance between prestige and unapproachable attitude? Adjusting the reference point to each group separately, will we now find that – both for the group of prestige brands and the luxury brands – a *relatively* more approachable attitude is rewarded in terms of greater consumer preference? As Figure 4.4 shows, the answer to this question is "yes" – and "no."

The distribution of brands on these two axes is distinctly U-shaped; there are brands with higher preference both at the low end of the unapproachable attitude spectrum and at the high end, while brands in the middle tend to have lower preference. Distinguishing between the previously defined prestige and luxury brands makes what is happening much clearer; for the former (black triangles towards the left of the graph) the more unapproachable the brands' attitude the less they are preferred. In contrast, for the luxury brands (grey triangles towards the right), the exact opposite is the case; brands like Rolex, Dior, and Tiffany's, which have the most unapproachable attitude, are on average twice as likely to be preferred as Bulgari, Dom Perignon, and Tag Heuer. Put very simply, for luxury brands being unapproachable is good.

Notwithstanding this apparently clear finding, we still have to find an explanation of why people might desire a brand that makes them feel that they are "not good enough." Probably, not everyone does; luxury brands are not intended for everyone; they are targeted at an elite group for whom "not good enough" might well mean something different to its plain meaning to

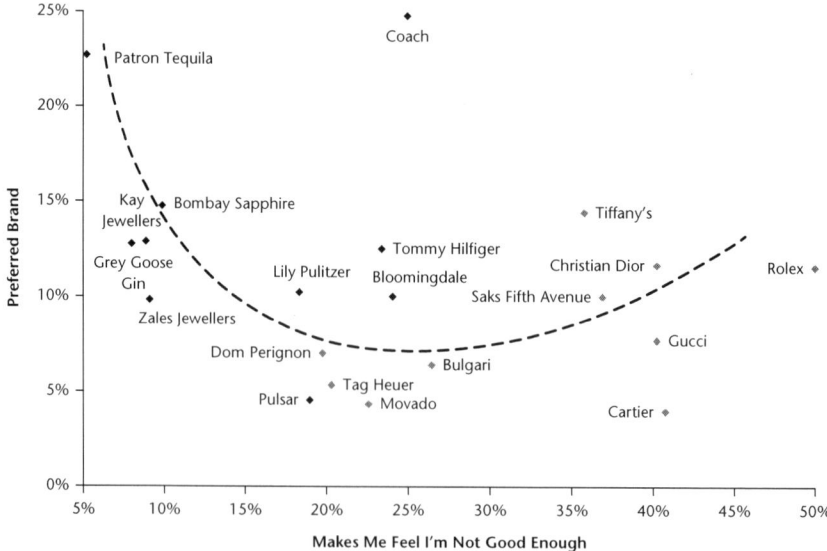

FIGURE 4.4 Prestige Brands – Preference and Brands' Attitude

everybody else. Whereas a non-member of the elite might internalize "not good enough" as a warning that the brand should be avoided as a means of preserving self-respect, the elite might see "not good enough" as an incentive for further self-improvement, and the brand therefore desirable as a means of achieving that improvement. What evidence do we have for these two hypotheses; that being made to feel "not good enough" is not good for everybody, and that it means different things?

The research for this study was conducted on a representative sample of the US population; in order to test the above hypotheses, we clearly needed to dig deeper by segmenting the sample into elites and non-elites. Elite status was determined behaviorally, as having ever purchased or used one or more of the ten luxury brands, a definition that qualified just 10 percent of the sample. The remainder were further segmented into "prestige brand users" – those ever having purchased or used one or more of the ten prestige brands (17 percent) – and non-users (73 percent). Examining the data under this microscope immediately confirmed the hypothesis that being made to feel "not good enough" is not good for everybody.

Figure 4.5 shows that those who say they prefer a brand that makes them feel "not good enough" are in fact a minority of a minority, just 19 percent among the prestige users and 32 percent among the luxury users. It is that minority which is accountable for the uptick of the U-shape in the chart in Figure 4.4. It is striking that, for luxury brand users, a brand that makes them feel "not good enough" is more attractive to them than one that doesn't have that attitude. In contrast, the preferences of prestige brand users go in the opposite – more intuitive – direction.

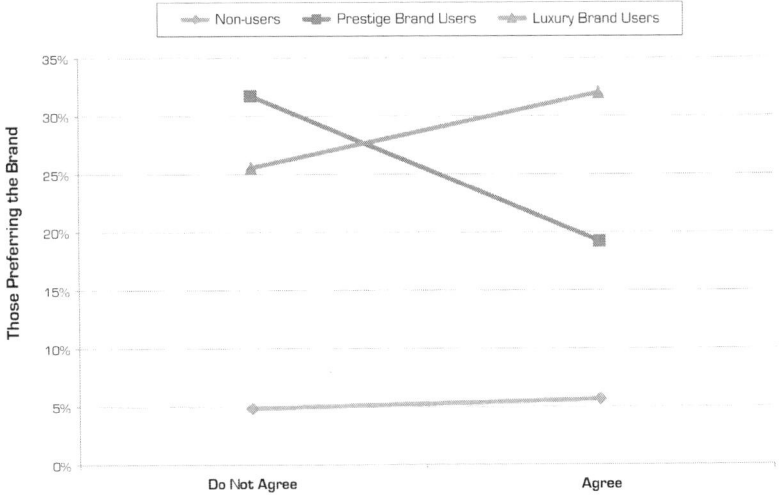

FIGURE 4.5 Preference for Brands with an Unapproachable Brand's Attitude

In order to answer the second question – what does being made to feel "not good enough" mean to elites and non-elites – we can examine the statistical correlation between describing a brand as "Makes me feel I'm not good enough" and other brands' attitudes on which the brands had been measured. These correlations are shown for the two different consumer groups – users of just prestige brands and users of the luxury brands – in Figure 4.6.

Not surprisingly, "not good enough" correlated highly with parameters such as "Unapproachable" and "Doesn't care what I think" for both groups of consumers. But from that point on the two lines part company; for prestige brand users, all the positive brands' attitudes correlate negatively with "not good enough"; for luxury brand users on the other hand, the two highest positive correlates of "not good enough" are "Recommended by people I care about" (approval by other people) and "Appreciates my business" (approval by the brand itself).

In fact, if we look at the brands' attitudes that are most closely associated with prestige itself, there is a net difference between the luxury brand users and those who use prestige, but not luxury brands. For both groups prestige is associated with *self*-related, or "inner-directed," brands' attitudes – "excites me," "provides a treat for me," "inspires me," "helps me express myself." However, for luxury

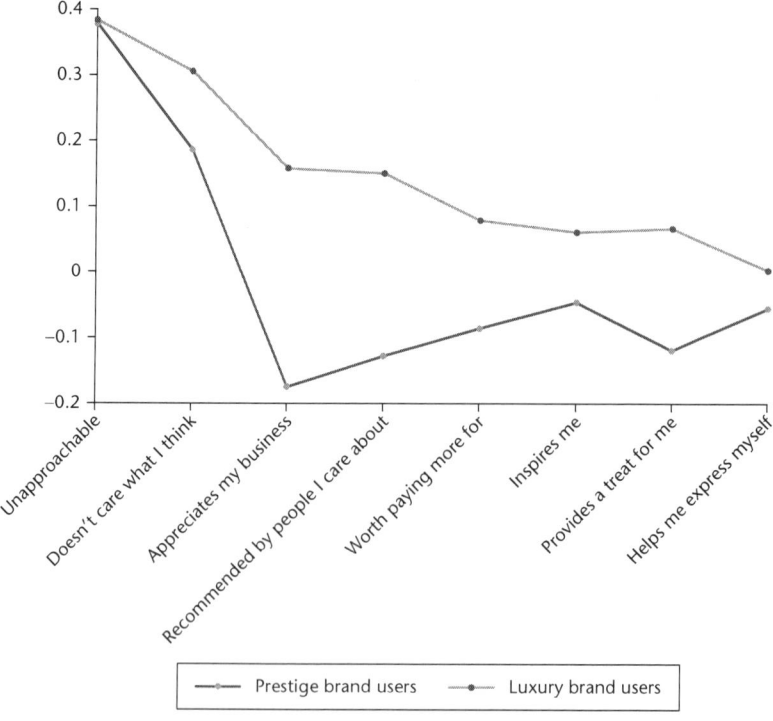

FIGURE 4.6 Correlations Between "Makes me feel I'm not good enough" and Other Brands' Attitudes

brand users, the emphasis on the *other*-related, or "outer-directed," brands' attitudes associated with prestige – "recommended by people I care about," "appreciates my business," "makes me look good to others" – is much higher.

For both groups, the relationship with prestige or luxury brands is about self-indulgence, making themselves feel good. But for the luxury brand user, it is also more about acquiring greater status. Wanting greater status implies a dissatisfaction with their current level of status and an aspiration to improve it; this is the reason why the apparently counter-intuitive "makes me feel not good enough" is a desirable brand attitude. The self-improvement that elites seek by aspiring to luxury brands is greater *approval*; approval by other people – and approval by the brand itself. If this sounds familiar, it is because that is exactly the conclusion we drew about the American Express brand back in its original, "unreformed" days. *"The American Express Card gives the member approval, an approval that recognizes the worthiness of the card member to share in the prestige, authority, and power of the American Express Card. Other people give card members approval, because the card approves of them."*

Although the balance between inner and outer-directed benefits is different, prestige brand users and luxury brand users both want approval. That brand relationship is the same, but the brand has to signal this relationship by diametrically opposite attitudes. For the prestige brand to appeal to a mass consumer, its attitude must be inclusive and approachable; in contrast, the luxury brand is expected by the elite consumer to be exclusive and unapproachable.

These days, very few brands remain the exclusive province of elites; the pressure for increasing shareholder value and the desire to exploit the growth of high net worth consumer markets, which drove American Express into the mass market, entice many luxury brands into reaching down to embrace a broader public. For a massifying brand – like American Express in the early 1990s – it becomes part of a broader question of how to manage the transition to a lower level of prestige. Although the core of the brand relationship – approval and status – may remain the same, massification inevitably means changing the signals – both brand image and attitudes – which establish that relationship. As excess value bleeds off to become "mere" added value – from luxury into the more mundane world of a prestige brand – the brand also has to shed its elite-oriented attitudes and become more welcoming.

Perhaps cognizant of the dangers of changing the nature of their brands' prestige, not all luxury brands have taken this route; some have preferred to maintain the integrity of their luxury status, and have managed their mass brand entry by other means. For example, the French haute couturier Hermès bought a stake in the more popular "street" values of the Jean-Paul Gaultier brand, after having hired Gaultier himself as their creative head. Alternatively, evolving a sub-brand architecture, like the different American Express cards, is one of the ways in which brand owners attempt to straddle the gap, by trying to keep a foot in the luxury camp while appealing to the masses. This same strategy has also been adopted by a number of American designers: Anne Klein and Anne Klein II, Ann Taylor and Ann Taylor LOFT (now more widely known just as "LOFT"). Unlike Hermès/Gaultier, sub-brands are not hermetically sealed off from each other, and the question is, in which voice does the brand actually speak – the mother brand's or that of the offspring? How convincing or confusing is it that the same mother brand has offspring with different values – or value – and different attitudes?

This is the dilemma of relationships with a complex brand, the brand that has to speak to different consumer audiences in different voices. It is one that is not unique to the prestige and luxury categories, and will be more broadly discussed in the following two chapters. In Chapter 5, we will examine the problems that have plagued the relationships of big financial service brands which try to serve different market sectors and in Chapter 6 we will see how large corporate brands navigate the waters of multiple brand relationships.

Note

1 Undoubtedly, the changed brand architecture in which the iconic Green Card now functions more like a regular credit card than as a "charge" card has also substantially influenced relationships with the umbrella American Express brand.

5

HOW BRAND RELATIONSHIPS MITIGATE CONSUMERS' RISK

Risk is often an important factor in shaping the types of relationship consumers look for with brands. Whenever the consumer is not easily able to evaluate the performance of the product up front, or when product failure could have serious consequences – material or otherwise – the consumer has to make a risk assessment. The stress of deciding which bar of soap to buy or even which restaurant to go to for a meal does not usually raise your adrenaline level too much; but the purchase of "high ticket" items – like computers or automobiles – is often associated with high levels of perceived risk and consequent anxiety. Many business decisions – because of the amounts of money involved, and the domino effect of product failure on the consumer's business or job – are made in favor of brands that are able to mitigate the risk.

Certain purchase decisions are inherently more "risky" than others. Generally speaking, the more money involved, or the graver the consequences of product failure for the decision maker, the greater the risk. In addition, the level of objective risk can be greatly modified by the consumer's own subjective perceptions of risk. Two different consumers may view exactly the same purchase decision very differently, depending on their individual assessments of the risk involved and – of course – depending on their previous experience of this type of purchase. For example, in the automobile and property insurance category there is an immense difference in attitude between customers who have never had to make a claim and those who have; the latter are much more sensitive to risk, and will usually be more likely to rely on a brand that somehow alleviates their perception of the level of risk. The insurance category is, of course, the archetypal risk category, as the "product" that the consumer purchases is actually the cancellation or mitigation of risk itself; it is, therefore, a useful starting point for the examination of all risk-mitigating brand relationships.

Brand Relationships in the Insurance Industry

In 1990, I conducted a study of customers' relationships with brands of auto insurance, in order to determine the most appropriate brand advertising strategy for a large US insurance company. We started by examining the relationships that customers *would like* to have with auto insurance brands in an ideal world. We discovered two rather different types of ideal brand relationship; one we called "Idealized Agent" and the other "Benevolent Authority." The characteristics of each are summarized in Figure 5.1.

Not unexpectedly, buying insurance – particularly auto insurance – is frequently anxiety provoking. The role of the brand in this situation should be to relieve that anxiety and provide reassurance. In both of the desirable relationships, consumers emphasized how important (reassuring) it was for the brand to be ethical and well-intentioned. In other respects, however, these two relationships are completely different, and it is easy to see how varying perceptions of risk – and the consequent levels of anxiety – would lead consumers in one direction or the other.

In the "Idealized Agent," a somewhat less anxious consumer is seeking a relaxed, reciprocal relationship founded on a basis of equality and shared interests. The brand should bring to the relationship its long experience (information), responsiveness (flexibility), as well as an attitude that implies interest in and concern for the welfare of the client. The customer wants the brand to be a channel of information and resources, but needs to retain his own independence and autonomy to make choices.

In contrast, for consumers whose perception of risk is more elevated, *expertise* (knowledge) is preferred to experience. A brand that accepts *responsibility* is more

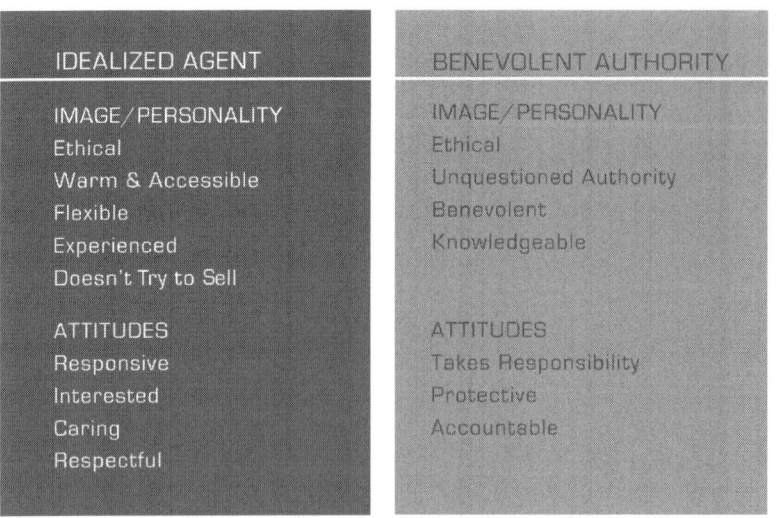

FIGURE 5.1   Ideal Relationships with Auto Insurance Brands

compelling than one that is just responsive to the client's needs. The consumer wants to see the brand's benevolence translated into an attitude of *protectiveness and accountability*, rather than one that is merely interested and caring. The "Benevolent Authority" is a more formal and dependent relationship. In it, the consumer would willingly trade off autonomy in return for a more authoritative and substantive commitment on the part of the brand. In this relationship, the consumer is looking for an authority figure to "tell" him how to look after himself.

Knowing which of these two different relationships is optimal can be crucially important for the insurance company trying to use its brand to obtain leverage with potential customers. The "Idealized Agent" represents a very convenient brand strategy for insurance companies, many of whom have a large agent force which can be made the focus and "hero" of the brand's market positioning. However, the greater the emphasis on the agent (idealized or otherwise) as the embodiment of the brand and protagonist of the brand relationship, the less opportunity there is for a more "corporate focused" relationship, like "Benevolent Authority."

The issue of agent vs corporation is not unique to the insurance category. As with any "tied" channel of distribution, it is a question of how integral a part of the brand the distribution should become. In almost every corporate situation there is the question of "what" should represent the brand in its relationship with the consumer, and in which voice the brand should speak. Can the same insurance brand be both a benevolent authority and an idealized agent? This is another form of the question that I asked in Chapter 4, in relation to brands that attempt to appeal to both elite/luxury and mass/prestige markets; how convincingly can the same brand speak to different consumer audiences in different voices? And this same question recurs in a slightly different form when we examine brand relationships in another financial services category.

Brand Relationships with Securities Companies

In this part of the financial services world, different perceptions and tolerance of risk also play a role in determining the type of brand relationship that is most comfortable for the consumer. Unlike insurance, for which the consumer pays money in order to minimize risk, the securities consumer *pays* with risk in order to maximize monetary gain. This puts a different perspective on the relationship requirements.

In the securities world, the less risk-tolerant consumer is a conservative investor who looks for a brand that appears to share this conservatism. The investor knows that no securities brand can take the responsibility for him, so he seeks to minimize risk by looking for a brand that knows how he feels and therefore will tend to act as he would act. These investors will, therefore, look for brands whose personalities and styles reflect their own, and whose attitudes are empathic and approachable. The conservative investor seeks a relationship based on close identification with the securities brand. In the aftermath of the financial world's 2008 paroxysms, it is now, of course, questionable whether investors – conservative or less so – can identify with any investment company brand – except perhaps the "Wizard of Omaha," Warren Buffet. Nevertheless, this remains an ideal relationship waiting for some investment brand to build.

The ideal relationship of more conservative investors is – paradoxically – similar to the ideal brand relationship of the less risk-conscious insurance customer – a relationship based on equality and shared interests, in which the brand brings its experience to the relationship. In contrast, more speculatively inclined investors can be compared to thrill seekers who look for someone who has characteristics that are very different from their own. Paramount among these characteristics is, of course, the expertise to maximize their return; in some way, this parallels the desire for the almost mythic/magical abilities that the risk-intolerant insurance buyer seeks. But whereas the latter is seeking the reassurance of a benevolent figure, the speculative investor expects the type of brand's attitudes that might otherwise be very injurious to a brand relationship – arrogance (or at least a lack of due deference) and little respect for the conventional and normative. As risk-tolerant investors are often very conventional people, these "desirable" attitudes often imply a lack of respect for themselves. Nonetheless, the relationship based on an admiration for and a pride of patronage of these "bad boy" brands is a very positive one.

To the extent that risk-intolerant insurance buyers are also more likely to be conservative investors – and those less concerned about insurance risk, more inclined to speculative investing – brand relationship requirements in insurance and securities are somewhat incompatible. They are summarized and compared in Figure 5.2.

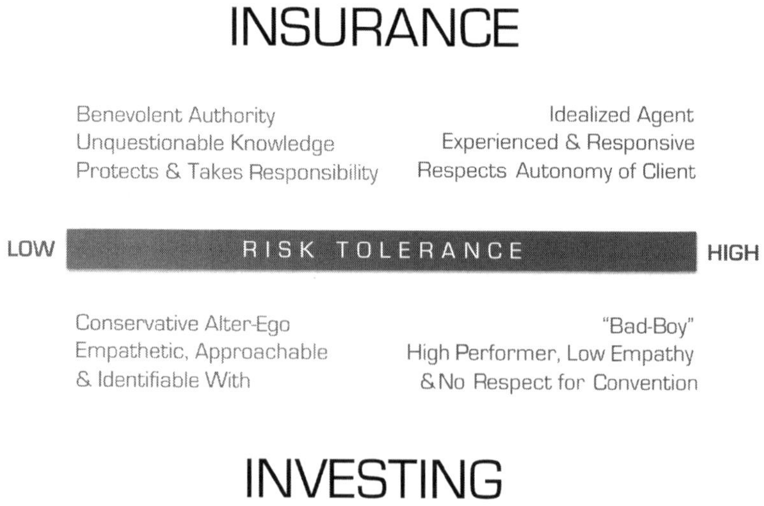

INSURANCE

Benevolent Authority	Idealized Agent
Unquestionable Knowledge	Experienced & Responsive
Protects & Takes Responsibility	Respects Autonomy of Client

LOW   **RISK TOLERANCE**   HIGH

Conservative Alter-Ego	"Bad-Boy"
Empathetic, Approachable	High Performer, Low Empathy
& Identifiable With	& No Respect for Convention

INVESTING

FIGURE 5.2 Risk Tolerance and Relationships with Financial Brands

Given the diametrically opposed nature of the products and the transactions – you pay for insurance in order to reduce risk, you pay with risk in order to increase financial returns – it is not surprising that the desirable brand relationships are so conflicting. But it does pose a problem for brands that are simultaneously present in both categories – a phenomenon which proliferated under the 1990s concept of "one-stop shopping" financial service brands. One brand attitude that is a fundamental requirement for all financial service brands – for both risk-averse and risk-tolerant consumers – is being seen to be acting in the client's interest rather than in the brand's self-interest. This is probably the single area in which security firms' relationships have most fallen short of expectations – and not just in the years since the implosion of the sub-prime market, Bernard Madoff, and the collapse of Lehman Brothers.

In the 1980s Prudential-Bache, a wholly-owned subsidiary of the Prudential Insurance Company of America, was packaging small investors' investments to create partnerships which bought oil wells, real estate, and aircraft. Most of these investments soon turned sour, but Prudential-Bache continued to market them, while lying about their value to existing investors in a decade-long fraud, which only emerged into the light in 1990; no single brokerage firm, banker, or trader destroyed the financial security of more people than Prudential-Bache Securities. What convinced many of these small investors to put their life savings, their retirement incomes, or homes at risk was undoubtedly the reassuring presence of the Prudential Insurance brand with its power to mitigate the perceived risk. When the Prudential brand was revealed to have been part of a scheme every bit as devastating to its investors as Bernard Madoff's,[1] there were ramifications for that brand's relationships with all of its customers – both insurance as well as securities. In their relationships with brands, people react with their gut more than the mind; never mind that there may have been "Chinese walls" separating Prudential-Bache from Prudential's insurance business; in most people's view, "The Pru" had been guilty of a great deal more than a lack of adequate oversight of its investment arm. Once again, the issue of conflicting expectations about the same brand in two roles proved to be a risk factor for its relationships with consumers in both. This will be further explored in Chapter 6, where I will delve more deeply into the relationships of complex corporate brands that serve different overlapping constituencies with the same brand name.

The Advantages and Risks of Brand Authority in Relationships

We have seen how an authoritative brand image combined with an appropriately benevolent brand attitude can work in categories where monetary risk is involved. How does this extend to other types of risk?

One of the most risk-prone areas for anyone is their health, yet more and more people are taking routine health matters into their own hands, rather than relying on the medical profession. A recent survey showed that as many as 35 percent of Americans prefer to self-medicate for headaches, colds, and flu and muscle pain; physicians also complain about the inroads that "Dr Google" is making into their territory. Doctors are, of course, one of the archetypal authority figures in most of our lives; so who – or what – is replacing that authority? An "Over the Counter" medication is associated with high levels of performance and personal risk –will it cure the condition? What happens to me if it doesn't work properly? Will there be any side-effects? How do people who self-medicate alleviate the anxiety created by whatever condition it is they are suffering from, and reduce the risk associated with the medication? Successful brands of OTC medication – in order to mitigate the consumer's risk – have to adopt the doctor's reassuring mantel of medical authority – and the responsibility. Tylenol, for example, has long dominated the OTC analgesics category and in spite of the entry into the OTC market of two previously prescription-only analgesics with strong branding (e.g. Advil and P&G's Aleve), Tylenol's share still stands at nearly 30 percent. For many users, the fact that they were first given Tylenol in hospital endowed the brand with a "medical" authority that they were prepared to depend on against all the performance claims of its competitors. But that is not Tylenol's competitive edge, as most of its competitors also invoke some of the same authority. Tylenol's advantage is its safety, the fact that it is recommended for children, for pregnant women, or for people whose stomachs can't take other types of analgesic. It is this that translates into an attitude of "taking responsibility," and which undoubtedly – together with some expert crisis-management – carried the brand through the Chicago tampering cyanide poisoning episode in 1982 relatively unscathed. Users feel they can literally depend on Tylenol to look after them.

A relationship of dependence is a very strong one, and leads to a high level of brand loyalty; but it can engender complacency about the brand relationship and a lack of sensitivity to changes in the brand's environment. Although many technology categories – such as computers or telecommunications – have historically been perceived as highly risky for many consumers, perceptions of risk evolve and change. This is the inevitable result both of the accelerating pace of technology and the *rate of change of customers' comfort level* with that technology. Consumers have all learned to expect change, and to expect that change will even things out. Even those who are "followers" rather than leaders in the adoption of new technology are now following earlier and more confidently than they did with the "new" technology that came earlier in their lives. What this means is that what was once high risk for the consumer can become less so, or that the size or the longevity of "risk-averse" consumer segments shrinks.

Brands which attempt to live just on their "heritage" – their historic strengths – without continuing to update it, slip all too easily into this trap. What worked once, now doesn't work. Many pioneers of technology have found that their names no longer inspire the automatic respect they once did. They have to continually "pay their dues" in terms of innovation and product excellence.

The old AT&T discovered that just because it (Bell Labs, that is) invented the transistor or developed the Unix operating system for computers, that did not buy it credibility with a new generation of consumers of technology. The less risk-averse consumer is generally very intolerant of the kind of authoritative brand positioning which "tells me what I should do"; they definitely want to make their own decisions, without surrendering any autonomy. A "we know best" attitude from the brand – far from being reassuring – will be regarded as presumptuous and inappropriate.

Relationships with the AT&T Brand

In a 1990 study of relationships with the AT&T brand – when it was still remembered as the original telephone company and still dominated long-distance calling in the US – a range of relationships – positive and negative – were identified. In many cases, the nature of consumers' relationships with AT&T depended on the type of products they bought from the company – whether they were just long-distance telephone customers, or whether they were also customers or potential customers for any of AT&T's business products. (In Chapter 6, there is a full description of this study in the context of relationships with corporate brands.) However, independently of this, relationships were substantially influenced by consumers' comfort level with technology, which corresponded inversely with the level of risk they perceived. Relationships between AT&T and consumers in three segments, each corresponding to a different level of comfort with technology, are shown in Figure 5.3.

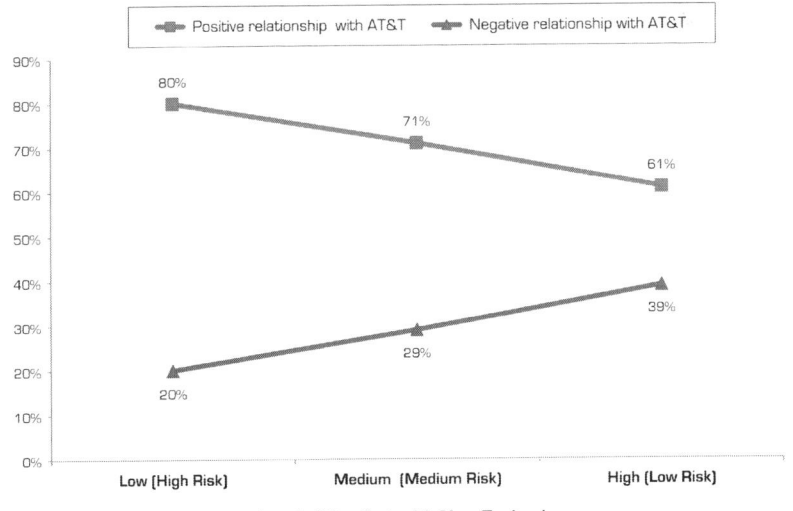

FIGURE 5.3 Attitude Toward New Technology and Brand Relationships with AT&T

Consumers who were not comfortable with new technology (high risk) were substantially more likely to have a positive relationship with the AT&T brand than those who were more comfortable (medium risk) with new technology; while the latter were more positive in their relationships with AT&T than the most comfortable (low risk) group.

In most cases, the negative relationships were related to what were seen as attitudes that were inappropriate to AT&T's current status and abilities. At best, while its past achievements were respected, the consumer was asking "what have you done for me lately?" More negatively, other consumers were not at all interested in AT&T's past achievements, and found AT&T's attitudes to be arrogant and self-satisfied.

As might be expected, people who are more comfortable with technology are younger, better educated, and more affluent. They also tend to own and use more "stuff" – both high tech and not so high tech. They are more critical of everything and everybody – particularly authority figures. They are basically the prime target for any leading-edge technology. None of this is surprising. However, what makes it more relevant for all categories of brands is that the early adopters are no longer just the millennials and their even younger cohorts; with each new wave of technology following more closely on the heels of the previous one, the high comfort group is reaching further and further "down" into the population. What this means is that authority is becoming a more and more difficult attitude to maintain. A case in point is the automobile industry: The market capitalization of Tesla – the maker of electric vehicles and space technology, which in 2016 sold less than 80,000 vehicles – recently exceeded that of General Motors, which sold over ten million in the same period. This shows where the smart money thinks that authority lies; and even though we have seen previous speculative bubbles, like the dot.com bust of 2000, consumers do often also follow the money trail. The general expectation is that Apple or Google – the new technology authorities – will lead the way in driverless cars, but perhaps consumers no longer require that type of authoritative reassurance; perhaps they will already have mentally discounted the risk, and will award the prize to a newer mold-breaking brand, such as Uber or another crowd-sourcer. We need to re-examine some of our familiar notions about the way new products diffuse through the population and – together with it – some of our ideas about appropriate brands' attitudes.

The Universality of Risk as a Factor in Determining Brand Relationships

Although I am not yet quite ready to generalize the discussion of Consumer Brand Relationships – Chapter 6 deals with relationships in one more specific type of category, corporate brands – I cannot conclude a chapter on risk without pointing out how universal is its influence on brand relationships. When

I worked at Ogilvy & Mather Advertising (1986–1991), it was the practice to build a consumers' risk assessment into every advertising strategy document, dealing with three types of risk:

- *Performance risk*; the risk of the brand's product performance being below expectation
- *Social risk*; the risk that using or purchasing the brand might have adverse social consequences
- *Self-image risk*; the risk to one's own self-regard as a result of using the brand.

In my experience since then, all these risks are still relevant, but there is an inter-dependence among them that needs to be considered. Specifically, performance risk and self-image risk are closely related; if the consumer is concerned with the risk of under-performance, then they will also perceive a self-image risk – "what if I make a bad choice." Conversely, there is also the reward for making a good choice; if the product performs satisfactorily, then that affects the consumer's self-esteem in a positive way. That coupling of performance risk and self-image risk is at the heart of a powerful brand relationship that I call "Reinforcement" – the intersection of perceived performance (brand image) with perceptions of how the brand makes me look (brand's attitude). I will deal much more thoroughly with Reinforcement, one of the "Universal" Brand Relationships, in Chapter 7.

Social Risk has always been a factor in those purchases where brand choice is "public"; the car you drive around in, the brand of clothes you wear, the brand choices you make for other people – either in the form of gifts or in business purchasing decisions. You put yourself "out there" and make a statement about yourself with these brand choices. Today – thanks to the internet and social media – the arena in which social risk is in play has vastly expanded; any interest you show in a brand on the internet, every purchase you make there, becomes "public" to a horde of other players, many of whom will then bombard you with ads for brands they perceive as similar to the ones you have shown interest in; in a way, your future brand choices become at least influenced by the choices you have made in the past. Beyond this, there is now a voluntary factor in publicizing brand choice decisions; social media has turned every brand choice into an opportunity to express oneself, to make a statement, to create and seek out other members of "brand communities." So the brands you like or love – for whatever reason – now also have to be brands that express who you are; they become part of your identity. I have referred in Chapter 1 – and demonstrated there with data – to the inadequacy of brand "love" (meaning the consumer loving the brand) as a stand-alone motivation for consumer behavior; the consumer's love for the brand must be in some way matched by a response from the brand. One such response is when the brand enables and facilitates the consumer's self-expression; the combination of brand love and consumer self-expression defines another important brand relationship: "Identification." Risk – social risk, in this case – is thus also at the heart of another of the Universal Brand Relationships, which are the topic of Chapter 7.

A recurrent issue in both this chapter and the previous one, concerning prestige, has been the "Janus" brand, the brand with two (and sometimes more) faces. Together with its different faces go different brand images, different brands' attitudes, different brand relationships. Economic theory tells us that price discrimination – charging different prices for the same good to different market segments – can only work when those segments are insulated from each other with no possibility of crossover from one to the other. So how does brand relationship discrimination work, when it is clear that – as in the case of insurance and securities or prestige and luxury – these different segments of the market are all fully exposed to one another? No brands face this dilemma more consistently than corporate brands, brands which are diversified both in their product line and the market segments they operate in, but which in all their various forms bear the corporate brand name. These brands are the topic of the next chapter.

Note

1 The Madoff fraud may have involved a higher amount of money, but those caught in it were for the most part not small investors, so fewer individual investors were involved. It is interesting to speculate whether what made Madoff such an attractive investment – apart from his seemingly reliably high returns – was a kind of vicarious "thrill-seeking" appeal of someone who has characteristics you do not have – and would not want in yourself.

6

RELATIONSHIPS WITH CORPORATE BRANDS

Corporations consist of multiple branded – or potentially branded – entities, which may include single products and whole product lines as well as subsidiary companies. The corporate brand itself may only be a financial or holding brand such as Berkshire Hathaway or United Technologies – familiar mainly to the investing and financial communities, but not generally associated with the company's product or services. This type of corporate brand essentially operates within only a single market – the stock market – with an undiversified product type – its stock or debt; as such, it does not fall within the scope of this chapter. The type of corporate brand that I am interested in here is diversified either in the type of products it sells and/or in the market segments it targets. This latter might be more correctly termed a corporate consumer brand inasmuch as the corporate brand name is associated by consumers with the company's products and services – even if these have their own brand names as well – and even if some of the products and services are not wholly owned by the corporation. Examples of such corporate brands are Apple, Ford, IBM, Sony, General Electric, Johnson & Johnson, American Express, and Virgin. Coca-Cola and Pepsi-Cola are consumer brands, but their corporate parents would not qualify as corporate consumer brands because many of the other products of the Coca-Cola Company and PepsiCo are not marketed to the consumer under the corporate brand name.

In addition to discussing two specific brand relationships that are fundamental to corporate brands, the other issue that I am concerned with in this chapter is the tension – potential or actual – between consumers' relationships with the corporate brand and their relationships with the individual product brands of the corporation. In each of the cases I deal with – automobiles, computing, and telecommunications products – the corporate brand is actively engaged in relationships with consumers. Thus, from the consumer's standpoint, the corporate brand acts as a "gate-keeper" to the individual products and brands of the corporation and as a guarantor of them; but it can also represent an obstacle in the way of engaging with them. From the corporation's point of view, the relationships of its corporate brand can be an envelope that encloses and defines the relationships of all its sub-brands and products with their consumers. If relationships with the corporate brand are positive and strong, then the products will benefit accordingly; if, however, there are negative relationships with the corporate brand, or if its relationships are inappropriate for the individual product brand, then the products will suffer. In the latter case, the corporate brand can become a straightjacket that confines its products and prevents them from developing their own ideal relationships. Sometimes, this requires radical action; for example, in 2003 the Philip Morris Corporation rebranded itself as Altria, in an attempt to free its non-tobacco subsidiaries – which at the time included Kraft foods – from the undoubtedly negative relationships that the majority of consumers now have with tobacco brands. More recently – and for different reasons – Google has renamed its corporate brand as Alphabet Inc., so that the vastly more diversified range of its current and future operations can develop brand relationships outside of those defined by the association with an internet search engine. Google has ceased to be a corporate brand.

There are instances in which individual product brands become so dominant – either deliberately or by happenstance – that they develop relationships that are independent of those of the corporate brand. This can work in a symbiotic way with the corporate brand; for example, the way that many people's relationships with the Apple corporate brand are totally mediated by their relationships with the iPhone brand. Alternatively, it can protect the individual product brand when relationships with the corporate brand are weak; I discuss in the next section examples of individual automobile brands, such as the Ford Thunderbird or the Chevrolet Corvette, for which the strength of their independent brand relationships enabled them to withstand the vicissitudes of their respective corporate brands' relationships. I also discuss, later in the chapter, the most clamorous case of a "rogue" individual product brand, the IBM PC, which effectively hijacked, and thereby inalterably changed for the worse, relationships with its corporate brand.

Relationships with Automobile Brands

In the automobile industry, the corporate brand versus product brand dichotomy – aka "marque versus model" – is a long-standing one, and is institutionalized by the system of distributing the products via tied dealerships. In other categories, the products of most other corporate brands can usually be purchased via independent channels of distribution, which means that they are at least exposed to the potential purchaser even if the latter does not initially have that brand within his or her consideration set. It is always possible, in the sales situation, for previous prejudices or lack of commitment toward a brand to be overturned. In the case of the automobile, however, the very act of entering the showroom presupposes, if not commitment to that corporate brand, then at least a willingness to consider it. The auto industry represents an extreme situation, both in its strengths and weaknesses. It is certainly not a model for all corporate consumer brands, but it is emblematic of the more general issues of consumers' relationships with corporate brands in other categories.

Relationships with a corporate brand are an "active" influence on behavior only at rather infrequent intervals; at other times they remain in the background. These relationships are based on a set of beliefs and brand's attitudes formed over a long period of time, some of them culturally or socially defined, rather than by individual perceptions. In order to have a positive relationship with a corporate brand, the individual has to feel comfortable that its values, attitudes, and behavior all "fit" with his own value system. This can involve everything from his feelings about buying "imported" cars to the "tone of voice" he detects in corporate advertising or other corporate communications, and to whether or not he respects the chief executive of the company. Because, like political candidates, large corporations have to please several constituencies, it is easy for them to become associated with values, attitudes, or political affiliations that are not shared by all of their consumers. Neither the corporation's nor the consumer's value systems change rapidly or frequently. As a consequence, consumers' relationships with corporate brands are not easily subject to change and are rather stable.

In contrast, relationships with the product can be much more volatile. The car owner is involved in daily "interaction" with the car itself, continuously experiencing its strengths and weaknesses, constantly reassessing what it does for him. Experience – driving a car, being an owner – is the main basis for the relationship with the car itself. Like any other product, someone decides to buy a car because s/ he believes it will satisfy their needs – both tangible needs as well as emotional needs for self-expression and self-image. This relationship is easily subject to re-evaluation and change. What happens when that change is a negative one?

When the consumer is disappointed with the product, there is a great advantage to having a strong relationship with the corporate brand. In the case of the car owner, it can act as a cushion against bad experiences or disillusionment with a specific car. Generally, consumers are much more tolerant of a product failure if they have a strong relationship with the corporate brand – hallowed myths about "lemons" or "Monday cars" are created to deal with the dissonance between the two. However, even strong corporate brand relationships are not invulnerable. A particularly bad experience with a product, or persistent or recurring problems, will eventually impact negatively on the relationship with the corporate brand. While generally the corporate brand relationship is resistant to change, a change for the *worse* unfortunately occurs more easily than one for the better. The particular negative experience that triggers such a change can then become elevated and generalized to the corporate brand level, and becomes an indelible part of *that* relationship. With an automobile brand, it is not at all unusual to hear someone say, for example, "I had a bad experience with a 'Chevy' twenty years ago, and I've never bought one since" or "they didn't fix the problem that caused those accidents because they don't care what happens after the cars leave the plant."

In contrast, the successful corporate brand can continually draw on the strength of its brand relationships to ensure the success of its products, or "sub-brands." In the auto industry, the way that market share is sustained is to build relationships between the corporate brand and car buyers that last throughout consumers' car-buying lifetimes, so that they keep returning to the brand every time they decide to buy a new car – on occasions deciding to buy "the new Ford" before even walking into the showroom. The key relationship quality that can lock the car buyer into this lifetime loyalty pattern is customer satisfaction.

To create customer satisfaction, the automobile brand has to be *customer-centered* (the brand's attitude), and *proactive* (the brand image/personality).

In today's highly competitive markets, being seen as "proactive" is often a necessary condition for creating customer satisfaction. Very few companies these days can count on customers beating a path to their door. Products and services must be *taken to* the consumer. People want to deal with companies they see as innovative, ambitious to succeed, ingenious in the development of new ideas, and hard-working. All this is necessary – but not sufficient. Being proactive on its own, however, can result in aggressive salesmanship – which is not the same thing as creating customer satisfaction.

The brand attitude that is crucial to securing real "Customer Satisfaction" in the relationship is demonstrating being *customer-centered*, rather than self-centered. Customer Satisfaction only results when customers perceive themselves and their needs as playing a central role in all this activity. Customers want to see all the aggressive energy as a *response to and support of* their needs. They want some sign that the corporation has listened to them – and responded appropriately. Otherwise it's just high-pressure salesmanship – something for which the automobile industry has been well-known.

In the mid 1980s the US automobile industry was on the defensive. The assault from Japanese imports, in particular, had reduced the share of market of the domestic producers to below 80 percent – then almost unthinkable. More than a decade of uninspired product development from the "Big Three" and poor quality control had helped turn the import foothold into a previously unthinkable wedge. The Japanese offerings, which a decade earlier had mainly penetrated the small car sector – the "soft underbelly" of the US market – had now established themselves firmly in the mainstream of full-size cars. The Honda Acura Legend and its cohorts from Toyota and Nissan had appeared, and were successfully challenging the US luxury marques. Throughout the 1970s and early 1980s the Japanese manufacturers were to be seen en masse at all the major auto shows in North America and Europe. They assiduously collected information about American made cars – took notes, covert photographs, and even bits of sheet metal – in their determination to match and beat the domestic makes. By 1986, "The most worrying thing is," as I heard one Detroit executive point out, "that they don't come anymore."

There were two encouraging developments in this otherwise dismal picture. Ford had emerged with a new corporate strategy, "Quality is Job #1," designed to actively reject and reverse the slipshod ways which had earned it a poor reputation both for design and quality. The decision to make quality a corporate strategy was a top management one; it was not just a slogan or an advertising campaign and was espoused with evangelizing zeal by senior managers in key departments throughout the company. Around the same time, in 1985, the Ford Taurus was launched – the new full-size car which replaced the generally disreputable "LTD." The Taurus – in addition to being the first new product of the new corporate strategy – was radically different from previous Ford designs; in fact, its decidedly European look – curved lines and comparatively little chrome – had given many US Ford executives nightmares.

The second counter-trend was in Chrysler – the "sick man" of the US Big Three. On the point of declaring Chapter 11 bankruptcy, the helm had been taken over by Lee Iacocca, an ex-Ford executive. His story has been well told (not least by Iacocca himself), so suffice it to say that by a radical restructuring of the company and some good product restyling, he had succeeded by 1986 in cutting costs and increasing sales. He bought the company enough financial breathing space and time for it to develop some badly-needed new products.

This was the background to an analysis of brand relationships in the US auto industry that I conducted in 1988. The Brand Relationship Map, Figure 6.1, shows the position of the major US and imported auto brands at that point in time.

As usual in the Brand Relationship Map, the horizontal dimension represents the brand image/brand personality component of the relationship and the vertical dimension the brand attitude.

Of the automobile brands considered, only Ford was seen at that time as unequivocally delivering customer satisfaction. A resurgent Ford was seen by many as reasserting the "proactive" values that made it an icon of American industry – innovative, entrepreneurial, and focused on the individual. In addition, consumers sensed that Ford was breaking away from the "Detroit knows best" philosophy that had dominated the American auto industry for a decade. New car designs (like the Taurus) were seen as arising out of Ford's listening and responding to the consumer.

Chrysler was also given high marks for proactivity. But it was seen as too "Chrysler-focused" to be responsive to consumer needs. The turnaround in the company's fortunes was admired, but the solution of its own business problems was seen as the sole motivation for this success. Car design was cited as evidence of – in Chrysler's case – a *lack* of responsiveness to the consumer. As one motorist put it: "Well, they fixed the company – but the cars are still the same."

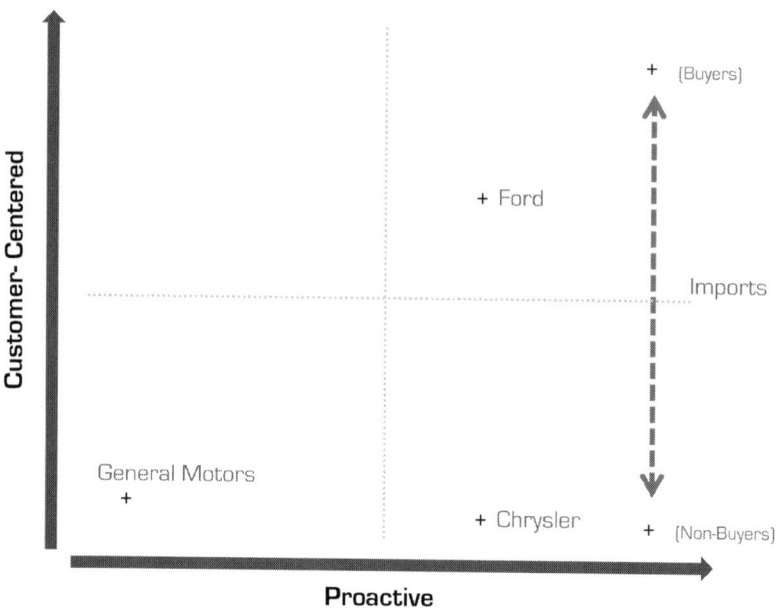

FIGURE 6.1 Automobile Brands' Relationships – Customer Satisfaction

General Motors fell down both in its image and its attitude. It was seen as being over-large, lacking in vitality, and bureaucratic. GM's attitude was seen as typifying "old-school Detroit" – continuing to design cars the way *they* think, oblivious to the consumer's voice.

While there was a good deal of consensus about the American auto brands, consumers' relationships with imported brands – particularly Japanese – were subject to conflicting emotions. Many consumers at that time were caught up in the "eternal triangle" of me, my car, my country, the feeling that if you cared about your country that had to affect your choice of automobile. Unfortunately, that created a conflict between their desire to be loyal Americans and their wish to have a satisfactory car ownership experience. Some of them had suppressed this conflict in a rueful and self-sacrificing way and were holding out, hoping for a renaissance of the American automobile. They saw the Japanese as the "new business culturists" who designed and produced outstanding cars because that was *their* culture, *not in response* to consumers' needs – certainly not American consumers. For others, however, the tension had become too great; not only had they bought an import, but they gave the feeling that they had forever severed their connection with American auto brands. For these consumers, in contrast, there was no doubt about the responsiveness of the import brand to them.

I will return to the automobile industry later in this chapter but, before moving on to other areas of corporate brand relationships, there is one post-script to the automobile case study, which I would like to add. This is to ask the question – which I alluded to earlier in the chapter – what is the brand? Is it the marque – Ford, Chevrolet, or Chrysler? Or, is it the specific model – the Taurus, the Corvette, the Le Baron? The question is important, as we have seen in Chapter 5 that the nature of the brand relationship can depend crucially on who or what is the brand's principal "agent" in its transactions with the consumer. I have no doubt – based both on my personal and my professional experience with auto brands – that the marque is almost always the prime mover in the establishment of brand relationships with the consumer. The "almost always" in the previous sentence is an important qualifier, because there are some notable exceptions – the (Ford) Thunderbird, the (Chevrolet) Corvette and the (Chrysler) Jeep. In each of these cases, the automobiles concerned embodied and preserved brand values and attitudes which once belonged to the parent corporate brand but which the latter had later ceased to represent. In at least one case, the manufacturer recognized this; for a period ending sometime in the early 1980s the "T-bird" did not display the Ford oval on its hood – it had literally, as well as symbolically, disowned its corporate parent. The point is that these exceptions "probe" (i.e. test) the rule, but do not disprove it.

Relationships with Computer Brands

In business decisions, brand loyalty is often based on trust. Going with a brand you can really trust makes the purchase decision a lot easier. But what does "trusting" a brand consist of? It is *not* just a question of reliability. Trust is created by reliability plus a sense of the brand's *involvement* with the buyer. The brand has to create a *personal* link with the individual customer, making the customer feel like more than just a sales statistic or a client code.

The second case history of relationships with corporate brands concerns the computer industry, and specifically addresses the issue of trust. The Brand Relationship Map in Figure 6.2 shows the position of various computer brands from an analysis carried out in 1989. It shows the extent to which the brands had built trust into their relationships with consumers, and the relative effects of its two components – reliability and involvement.

The positioning of IBM and Apple illustrates how trust can be achieved by different means. IBM's long-standing reputation gave to its image an unassailable credibility. Apple, on the other hand, while lacking the same degree of credibility – among corporate computer buyers – was perceived to know and understand its consumers much better.

Neither Compaq nor the other IBM clones achieved this same level of trust in their relationships. Compaq's reputation for technical excellence and for leading innovation in computer design gave it a credibility rating as high as IBM's. But Compaq was seen as being distant and aloof from the consumer. This perceived attitude of Compaq was at least in part due to its policy of distributing its

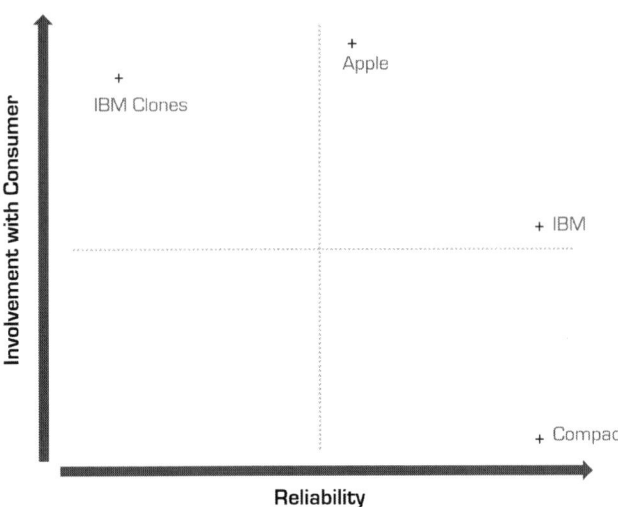

FIGURE 6.2 Computer Brands' Relationships – Trust

products only via added-value retailers; there was no direct contact between the corporation and the end customer. In contrast, the other clones – probably as a result of their direct marketing approach – were seen as being closer to, more knowledgeable about, more in touch with the consumer – but had the least credibility of all the brands.

In contrast to the case of the automobile brands, where the background leading up to the situation reflected in the brand relationships map was very germane, in this case it is what happened *afterwards* that is more relevant. At the time the relationship map was drawn up, the horizontal dimension – the brand's image for reliability – was an important component of the relationship – at least as important as the brand's attitude of involvement – and this was sufficient to keep many corporations loyal to IBM and Compaq. What happened around 1990 was the virtual collapse of the horizontal dimension as a differentiating factor between computer brands. Computer buyers – in corporations as well as private individuals – no doubt encouraged by the increasingly ubiquitous "Intel inside" stickers and slogans – started to believe that a chip was a chip, and that it made very little difference to the performance and reliability of the finished product who assembled them into a computer. When reliability stopped being a key differentiating factor between the brands, the trust relationship suddenly came to depend almost exclusively on brands' attitudes – that was the only difference consumers now had to go on.

In 1991, sales of Compaq plummeted, as buyers were no longer willing to pay the premium for what they now regarded as essentially the same product as any other brand. Compaq responded to this drastic situation by bringing their prices into line with the market – an essential short-term response – and, more vitally for the long-term health of the brand, by developing a totally new sales and distribution strategy which involved them more directly with the customer.

Trust in IBM was also weakened by the flattening of the reliability dimension, and this no doubt contributed to the crisis that subsequently hit the IBM brand and the IBM corporation. However, it was the radical change in another type of relationship – one that was unique to IBM – which was the major cause of the near demise of this corporate brand.

The question of how much prominence to give the individual product or service brand relative to the corporate brand is one of the most important issues in the management of any corporate brand. If the brand should become fragmented, and the different parts allowed to act as independent "agents," the relationship that consumers form with the dominant brand "agent" will influence their relationships with all the other parts of the brand. This is exactly what was allowed to happen to IBM, one of the most venerable and iconic of brands.

Until the mid 1980s, when the mainframe computer began to yield its hold on corporate computing to the PC, the IBM brand was unassailable. IBM always took complete responsibility for the satisfactory implementation and functioning of its mainframe computers. The world-renowned IBM sales force embodied this key brand attitude of taking responsibility. They helped build a relationship, between the customer and IBM, of dependence. This was at the root of the widely accepted maxim "No one ever got fired for choosing IBM." Choosing IBM took the risk away from the customer – by taking the responsibility away. As with the "benevolent authority" in the insurance category, the consumer was prepared to give up his own decision-making autonomy in return for the security offered by the IBM brand. The point was that the customer did not buy machines from IBM; what they bought from "Big Blue" were solutions – guaranteed, risk-free solutions to business problems.

Until the advent of the PC, there was only one brand – the Corporate IBM brand. With the launch of the PC through independent retail channels, an IBM machine (an "agent" of the corporate brand) itself for the first time effectively also became a brand (and the machine – unlike the brand – was all too fallible). The relationship with the PC brand was different; the customer now had to deal with the retailer/distributor for support; IBM no longer "took responsibility" for everything. The strength of the pre-existing brand relationship was sufficient to give IBM a dominant share of the PC market initially. However, as the basis for the relationship shifted away from mainframe computing to personal computer products, so dependence on "Big Blue" – and its market share – waned. In addition to the more general brand developments in the computer industry described above, which occurred at the same time, the loss of the unique relationship of dependence on IBM spelt the end of the IBM brand as we knew it.

Relationships with a Complex Corporate Brand – the Case of AT&T

One of the most important differences between a corporate brand and other types of brand is in the nature of "the consumer." When the company is the brand, there are far more critical points of contact between the brand and its consumers. "Consumers" range from the company's own employees, through its customers, to legislators, regulators, and the community at large. These points of contact are not isolated from each other – they overlap and interact. Although as marketers we may find it convenient to divide up our brand's activities – between corporate communications, business-to-business advertising, consumer advertising, and promotion – we have to be aware that our various audiences will not accommodate us by partitioning their minds and tuning in to only the appropriate set of messages.

The case of AT&T at the end of the 1980s dramatically illustrates a corporate brand in just such a situation – some six years after the anti-trust decision that had forced the break-up of "Ma Bell" and the divestiture of its local telephone services. The AT&T brand not only had relationships with different consumer segments, but those relationships needed to support a very varied selection of products and services, catering to different types of consumer needs. For many people AT&T was still "the phone company" even after its forced break-up – and for the majority of private telephone users at that time it was still their only long-distance telephone carrier. However, for many business people it was also one of several competing vendors for telecommunications equipment and services. In the old days, before the divestiture of its local telephone companies, equipment had been very much a sideline business that grew organically out of AT&T's huge customer base. In the post-divestiture world, business equipment and associated services was a key plank in AT&T's offering to the non-domestic customer; and, unlike in the past, the customers for these products were not necessarily from AT&T's telephone service customer base.

Trying to use a single brand to appeal to a number of different audiences had the effect of producing a remarkable disparity in the style of the brand's communications. At the time, AT&T had yet to find a new way of addressing private telephone consumers that was appropriate to an environment in which it was not the only long-distance carrier, and had to compete for the first time with others. Consequently, the images that were still in consumers' minds, and that set the tone of their relationship with the brand, were those of the long-running – pre-divestiture – "Reach Out and Touch Someone" campaign. This was a very "emotional" message, whose objective – in the monopolistic pre-divestiture situation – was simply to encourage people to make calls.

On the private consumer side of its business – with the advantage of being the incumbent long-distance carrier – AT&T could afford to take some time to figure out how to address the slow erosion of its customer base. However, in the area of business equipment and services, AT&T was engaged in a tough no-holds-barred battle for market share with a number of formidable domestic competitors like IBM and Northern Telecom, as well as any number of imports. As part of this struggle, AT&T was addressing its business customers – large corporations and small and medium-sized businesses – with various hard-selling campaigns, which included many messages designed to "scare" them into choosing AT&T equipment. (Some of these campaigns prompted advertising commentators to write about a new genre of advertising, which they dubbed "Slice of Death.") Although this style of advertising – which was such a departure for AT&T – met with success in some quarters, it also generated no little resentment for what was seen as an attitude that ignored the real interests of its customers.

A business decision-maker – when not a business person – may be just a regular long-distance customer of AT&T. How was he supposed to feel about these radically divergent sets of attitudes which AT&T was displaying toward him? And what about all the regular residence long-distance customers who just happened to tune in to one of the campaigns directed at businesses? Was this still the AT&T they knew and loved? More importantly, was this the AT&T that they thought loved *them*? What effect did this have on the type of relationships which AT&T had with its consumers?

In a study of AT&T's brand relationships in 1989, conducted across all of AT&T's customer groups, I identified six different types of relationship – both positive and negative. All of AT&T's customers – whether business or consumer – formed a relationship based on what they perceived to be the dominant attitude of the brand. Here are two of the types of relationship identified – one positive, the other negative – resulting from two very different perceptions of the brand's attitudes:

Relationship 1 – Identification/Partnership

- Key Brand Personality Characteristics; down to earth, reliable
- Key Brand's Attitude; involvement.

In this relationship, AT&T seems to be saying to the consumer: "You and I are very similar. We are hard-working, honest, and reliable. We can count on each other." The brand here is perceived to be an intimate of its consumer. The resulting relationship – characterized by a high degree of identification with the corporate brand – was found both among the customers of its consumer goods and among some business-to-business customers.

Relationship 2 – Disrespect

- Key Brand Personality Characteristic; aggressive energy
- Key Brand's Attitude; self-centered.

In this relationship, consumers heard AT&T saying: "I don't need to listen to you. I am AT&T, and that is enough for you to know." AT&T here was perceived to be completely lacking in what we have defined as supportiveness, customer-centeredness. This relationship – which needless to say was not characterized by a high degree of customer satisfaction – was only found among business-to-business customers of the corporation. It was a negative relationship characterized by a lack of respect for AT&T based on its professional and business attitudes.

Figure 6.3 illustrates the behavior of these two relationship segments, in terms of their purchase and use of AT&T's business and residential products.

Those consumers – private and/or business – with whom AT&T enjoyed the positive relationship were 20 percent more likely than average to have AT&T as their domestic long-distance carrier and the companies they owned or worked for (whose purchasing decisions they influenced) were 11 percent more likely than average to use AT&T equipment – anything from small business telephone systems to major switches. In contrast, business customers, consumer products customers, or both – those who perceived that AT&T took no notice of their needs – were less likely to use AT&T across the board. The disrespect relationship, created by the perceived indifference of AT&T to the views of its business customers, not only depressed their purchasing of its business products by 36 percent *but also had a similar effect on their having AT&T as their home long-distance carrier* – which we might have assumed to be immune to such business-related attitudes.

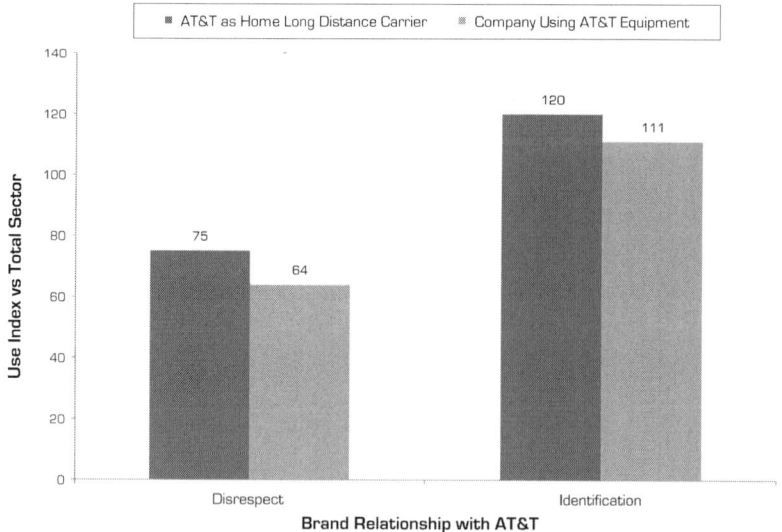

FIGURE 6.3 Influence of AT&T's Brand Relationships Across Sectors

Research on the relationships of corporate brands has demonstrated this point time and again; consumers form a single, unitary relationship with a corporate brand, a relationship that reaches into and influences every point of contact between the individual and the company. Having a positive relationship positively influences brand preferences across a range of decisions – business and private – while having a negative relationship – as illustrated by the AT&T case – often has an even larger downside effect. Further, as illustrated by the case history quoted above, we have found that relationships are forged at the most critical point of contact – the point of contact where the consumer's perception of *risk* is highest. The manager who has a negative business (higher risk) relationship with a corporate brand is likely to avoid choosing that company's products or services at home – independently of their merits or those of the competition. This is yet another example of how risk must be factored negatively into the equation defining consumers' relationships with brands.

Trust – Revisited

The three cases discussed in this chapter were all based on studies of brand relationships in the second half of the 1980s. They were also all based on the relationships with the specific target groups of each corporation's products. In 1994, I had an opportunity to revisit these corporate brands' relationships in the context of a more general examination of the relationships of a broad range of corporate brands – from a variety of different categories – with the "American Consumer" in general.

As discussed at the beginning of this chapter, aspects of consumers' relationships with a corporate brand are not always determined by the individual interactions between the two; certain types of perception – either of the brand's personality or of its attitudes – may well be conditioned by social or cultural norms and prejudices. One of the most obvious ways in which this might happen is in relation to the national origin of the corporation. Because the health of the domestic automobile category, for example, has been so closely identified with America's general economic wellbeing, there is – or was – among many sections of the population a strong "buy American" sentiment that could transcend individual preferences and experience. As described earlier, this was certainly very evident in research in that sector in the mid to late 1980s. The question was, what had happened since that time?

Having penetrated the American market, the Japanese auto manufacturers set about trying to *be* American companies – with US manufacturing plants, sponsorship of American cultural and sporting events, and identification with American icons. Their efforts were certainly a great deal more than just respect for the "domestic content" quotas, which they were obliged by law to observe; they represented a real attempt – motivated by enlightened self-interest – to transcend national stereotypes.

In the study of brand relationships that forms the last case history in this chapter, the corporate brands chosen for inclusion were deliberately diverse – auto brands and non-auto brands, Japanese and American. The objective was to see to what extent brands' attitudes were constrained by their national origins or were able to transcend them. The first Brand Relationship Map, Figure 6.4, shows the positioning of the eight corporate brands in the study in terms of Trust.

As we saw earlier, Trust is created by a perception of reliability plus a sense of the brand's *involvement* with the buyer. First, it can be seen how the images of the Honda and Toyota brands for Credibility and Reliability were still superior to both of the US auto brands'; but added to this, the efforts of Toyota and Honda to become American brands – to be seen as involved with the US consumer – had by the mid 1990s put them virtually at the same level as Ford, ahead of General Motors, and had won them a place ahead of such pillars of the American corporate establishment as IBM. The strength in the attitudes of these two Japanese brands was no longer just the opinion of people who had bought Japanese autos – as it had been when the previous research was conducted in the 1980s – this was a general perception across the whole of the US population. I suspect that this achievement owed less to the efforts of the corporate PR activities than it did to the flagship products of these two corporations – the Toyota Camry and the Honda Accord. In 1994, the year of this study, eight in every one hundred cars bought in the USA was either an Accord or a Camry; the only other car that approached the sales of each of these two models was the Ford Taurus. These best-selling cars, which over the previous 20 years had become so familiar and well-loved by so many Americans, cannot have failed to extend their aura of reliability and attitude of involvement to their respective corporate parents.

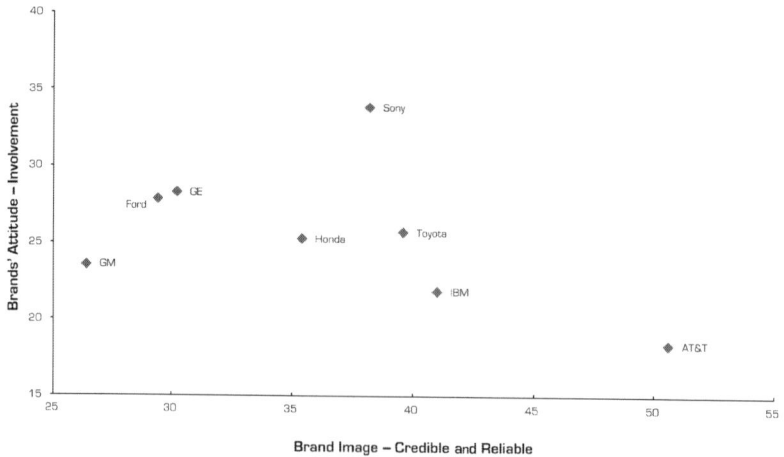

FIGURE 6.4 Corporate Brand Relationships – Trust

This seems to be the reverse of the process described earlier in this chapter, whereby the corporate brand's relationships act as the springboard for those of the products. Does this mean that these two cars represent further "exceptions to the rule" (that the automobile marque is the principal agent of the brand, not the model) in addition to the ones noted earlier in this chapter? I do not believe that either the Camry or the Accord had become quasi-independent brands like the Thunderbird or the Corvette. Unlike in those cases, where there was an apparent divergence between the values and attitudes of the products and those of the corporation, the Honda Accord and the Toyota Camry are cases of old-fashioned long-haul brand creation, in which a manufacturer's products have won a reputation for consistent quality and reliability, and thus created similar expectations about all the products of that manufacturer. The Camry and the Accord – because of their ubiquity and longevity on the American domestic scene – were the brand agents, which created an attitude of involvement, and hence built the relationship of trust that we see now. But the products were clearly seen as ambassadors of their corporate brands, rather than as independent agents.

Sony – a third Japanese corporate brand (although how many people in the heyday of the Sony Walkman thought of it as such?) – had exceeded even the achievements of Toyota and Honda in terms of its brand relationships. Again, it was the ubiquity of its products and the seamless place they then occupied in the fabric of so many Americans' lives that created the attitude of being involved. AT&T is another matter; what could be more ubiquitous than "The Phone Company"? The relative weakness of the AT&T brand's involvement attitude is an important warning that not all mass brands can create or maintain this attitude merely by being ubiquitous; their ubiquity has to be the result of consumers' consent, not their conscription. Consumers have to actively *want the brands in their lives* – not be obliged to, because of an absence of choice. A notable "epiphany" that I experienced when I was working with the AT&T brand is that competition is an essential precondition for brand loyalty; that the process of building loyalty to a brand comes about as a result of the consumer being able to make choices. After deregulation of the long-distance telephone market in 1984, many of AT&T's long-distance customers left that brand when other long-distance options became available – not because they were dissatisfied with AT&T, but simply because they could. A similar phenomenon occurred with other utility companies – gas and electricity suppliers – as those markets became increasingly deregulated in the 1990s. Brand loyalty can only be forged in the crucible of competition. Trust, as part of the consumer's relationship with a brand, is an important contributor to brand loyalty, and trust too can only emerge from consumers' choice – it cannot be mandated by the corporate brand, either by restricting competition or by telling consumers to "Trust me."

The problems of AT&T are again highlighted in Figure 6.5, which deals with Customer Satisfaction, which together with Trust is one of two recurrent themes in relationships with corporate brands.

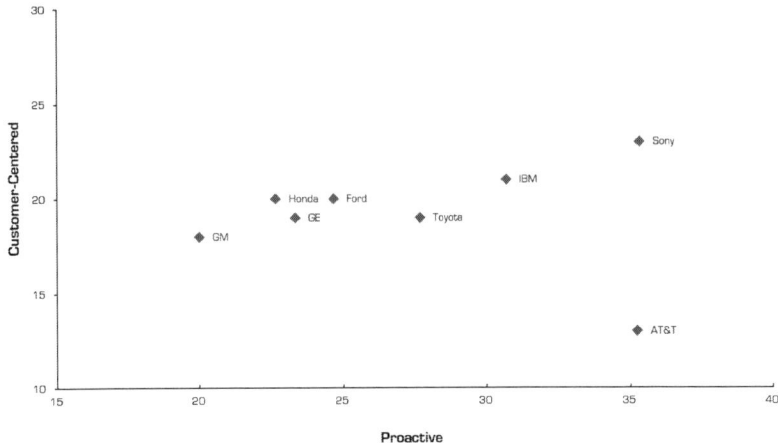

FIGURE 6.5 Corporate Brand Relationships – Customer Satisfaction

In this relationship, the key brands' attitude is customer-centeredness. Despite its reputation for innovation, which is an important contributor to its proactive image, AT&T was still seen to be more driven by its *own* interests than by those of its consumers. The relationship between an individual consumer and a corporate brand is intrinsically an unequal one. It therefore requires a lot of effort on the part of the brand to give the individual a feeling that their interests count. When the consumer's purchase of a product from the corporation – like an automobile or even a smartphone – is a "big ticket" item, the relationship is put under even greater strain. The consumer sees him or herself making a very large commitment to the brand – in time as well as money – and would like to see in return a very tangible effort on the part of the brand to match that commitment. In order to offset what is otherwise a sense of weakness, of loss of control – even when their attitudes toward the brand are positive – consumers need to feel "listened to." Being listened to requires doing more than just providing a product that consumers like – or even love; it means producing a product that is – at least in part – developed or adapted based on an active consideration of their needs. How to provide this apparent personalization of the product experience is one of the key challenges for the corporate brand. In the 1980s, Ford Taurus buyers really believed that this car was a sign of Ford "listening" to them; it was just what many had been yearning for – a complete break from Detroit product design, but designed in Detroit. Much more recently, lovers of Apple's iPhones saw the iPhone 6, with its larger screen, as a corporate response to their needs. In fact, it represents an unusual case of Apple responding to and following competitive pressure; but such is the identification of Apple's iPhone customers with the brand that the new model was seen as resulting from their needs rather than Apple's.

In this last case study, I deliberately set out to compare corporate brands from a number of different product categories – comparing Ford with Sony, IBM with Toyota, etc. The two brand relationships shown here are so fundamental to the issue of corporate branding that they transcend the particularism of specific product categories. It is possible to go even further in this process of generalization and identify a set of Universal Brand Relationships that are common to all product categories – corporate brands, packaged goods brands, service brands, and even "celebrity" brands. In all product categories, there are a set of common processes involved in brand-building; bringing new users into a brand's franchise and keeping them there, encouraging brand preference and loyalty, supporting a higher price and bigger margins, making more profit and – ultimately – building a branded business that financial markets value highly. Each of these processes is mediated by consumer brand relationships, and the set of Universal Brand Relationships comprises the tools needed to build a generalized model of the connections and pathways between the relational brand and a successful branded business; they are the topic of the next two chapters.

7

UNIVERSAL BRAND RELATIONSHIPS

Universal brand relationships are not a replacement for the category-specific brand relationships that have been the subject of this book up to this point; they serve a different purpose, which is the generalization of the lessons learned about the relational brand over the last 30 years, and the building of a quantitative model of consumer brand relationships. Universal brand relationships have been identified using the same relational philosophy and methodology employed in the study of category-specific brand relationships. They do not arise in a vacuum; they are just broader "envelopes" into which we could classify more specific brand relationships, and they are informed by the knowledge and understanding that has been gained of category-specific analogues. There is a trade-off, because generalization inevitably entails a loss of precision and focus, so that universal brand relationships may not be as useful as category-specific ones for fixing the relationships of brands in a specific category.

Over the last few years my business partner, Ed Lebar and I have been building a generalized model of Consumer Brand Relationships, based on the principles outlined in the earlier chapters of this book, and refined by the experience acquired in the many individual product categories that I have worked on. Ed was for many years the Managing Director of Young & Rubicam's BAV – BrandAsset Valuator – division, which has collected the world's largest database of consumer-derived brand information. As such, Ed has a unique experience of comparing brands across multiple categories and modeling the relationships between consumers' evaluations of brands and macro brand data, such as sales, profit margins, and financial valuations. I got to know Ed when I worked with him as a consultant to BAV for about five years.

We have to date conducted three large-scale studies in multiple categories – one in the USA and two in Latin America. The observations and analyses presented in this chapter are largely based on those studies. In spite of the difference between, say, the USA and Mexico, our findings display a high level of convergence in terms of the fundamentals that underlie consumers' relationships with brands in these two countries. In particular, we have found convergence in the number and type of Consumer Brand Relationships that are relevant across multiple categories, and in the two components of these relationships – consumers' perceptions and their projections of brands' attitudes.

The data used in this chapter and the one that follows is from the USA study, conducted in 2012. This was a large-scale internet survey of 48 brands in eight different categories conducted on a representative sample of over 1,500 consumers, each of whom were questioned on 16 brands. The survey yielded a total of some 22,000 observations of brands, of which about 12,000 observations were from previous month users of the brands concerned, and 10,000 from non-users. Brands were evaluated on the following series of issues:

- familiarity
- perceptions of brand image and personality
- brands' attitudes
- brand "touch" points (advertising, websites, social media, etc.)
- brand usage and consideration
- overall brand evaluations
- other brand-related behavior.

As described in Chapter 2, the relational model is not based on the central assumption of additive models – that a brand's strengths can compensate for its weaknesses. In the Relational Brand model, relationships are composed of two essentially different components that interact in a non-compensatory manner; a brand relationship has emergent properties, meaning that a positive relationship is more than the sum of its parts (and a negative one is less); so the function relating brand relationship strength to the strength of the two components has to reflect those properties. This principle is true of Universal Brand Relationships as well as of specific category relationships.

How many universal brand relationships are there? Comprehensive multi-category studies of brands normally identify between six and eight different dimensions of consumer perceptions and usually a slightly lower number of distinct dimensions of consumers' projections of brand attitudes. In theory, the number of possible brand relationships is determined by the combinatorial possibilities of the two sets of component dimensions. In practice, of course, not all such combinations have a relational logic to them, and not all of them have emergent properties (I discuss the technical aspects of defining and measuring emergence in the appendix). Using these two criteria, I have identified a set of five brand relationships that I refer to as the five "universal" relationships – universal because they emerge from measurement across multiple product categories.

1. Reinforcement

Reinforcement is a powerful relationship: The basis for it is both the customer's satisfaction with what s/he sees as the superior performance of the brand, and the feeling that the brand has made him/her better and smarter – in his/her own eyes and in those of others. Both are integral to the relationship, and the connection between them works both ways; because the brand delivers the desired – or expected – performance, it makes the customer feel good; and because using the brand makes the consumer feel good, it must – to avoid cognitive dissonance – be seen as a high-performing brand. The consumer's perceptions and the way the brand makes the consumer feel are mutually reinforcing. It is this two-way causality that strengthens the consumer's attachment to the brand. In reality, the brand's performance need only be "good enough" to avoid any shortfall from the customer's expectations; the perception of superiority may in fact only be the result of the brand engendering feelings of high self-esteem – "You did well. You made the right decision. You are smart."

Reinforcement is an important relationship in most product categories, but particularly so frequently purchased packaged goods categories. It is the engine that solidifies brand loyalty in many HBA (Health and Beauty Aid) and cleaning product categories. In these performance-focused categories, doing a good – or good enough – job is not sufficient; the brand also has to convince the user that s/he is – or would be – a better, smarter person by using the brand.

2. Identification

Identification is about loving the brand and loving oneself. The consumer likes the brand a lot because it reflects and expresses his/her own values and aspirations. The brand therefore helps the consumer express him/herself without conscious effort; "it's who I am; it makes my life easier." The classic case of identification is the – more often male – motorist's relationship with his brand of automobile; but it is also very evident with digital devices; most people are either iPhone people or Android and before that they were either Apple or PC people. Identification is a very important element in relationships with the Apple brand. There is a degree of mutuality here too; brand love and self-love are conjoined; if you love a brand so much, it should love you too; although that is not always the case.

We saw in Chapter 1 that only in 50 percent of cases do brands that are liked a lot or loved give an emotional response to the consumers that like or love them. We also saw that when the consumer did project an emotional response from the brand there was higher brand usage, stronger brand loyalty, greater evaluation of brand worth, and a generally much higher level of involvement with the brand on the internet and in social media. However, developing the appropriate brand attitude for Identification – one that makes the consumer feel loved – is not as straightforward as for other brand relationships. The kind of parameters that we use to measure this brand attitude are not the same as the ones that create it; asserting that "we let you be yourself" or "we help you express your hopes and wishes" is likely to leave many consumers at best indifferent. So what is the appropriate brand attitude for creating a loving brand?

It turns out that what makes a brand seem loving varies by product category (and within category, by individual brands) but there is one essential constant across all categories; feeling that the brand is "there for me" – that it responds to "my needs," has "my interests" at heart – is a factor that is invariably influential in making a brand seem like a loving brand. It is not the romantic love or white-hot passion that we are familiar with from interpersonal relationships; the consumer is very consumer-centered when it comes to feeling loved.

One last point about Identification; I have pointed out in Chapter 2 that not all people are capable of self-love; and in Chapter 5 we saw that there are high-risk categories – like insurance or investment – where many people prefer relationships with brands that are not like them. In both these instances, identification is not an important relationship.

3. Role Model

In Chapter 6, I described how the relationship of Trust in computer brands radically changed when consumers rather suddenly ceased to perceive any meaningful difference between the reliability of different brands; Trust became totally dependent on brands' attitude of involvement or intimate knowledge of the customer. In the intervening years, things have moved on – and not just in the category of digital devices and services. Brands – corporate brands in particular – have discovered a new dimension by which to differentiate themselves in the perceptions of customers; Brand Charisma. Charisma is a progressive style of leadership and innovation, which enthuses and excites people. Apple, of course, having matured from its insurgent mold-breaking role, now epitomizes the charismatic leader; but there are other brands, like Starbucks and Google, which have also notably achieved this distinction. However, as with reliability, charisma by itself is not sufficient to create a strong brand relationship; the brand also has to challenge, inspire, and encourage the customer to lift their game to a higher level, to be progressive and innovative too; the brand must be a mentor. Whereas Trust depends on the brand's attitude of involvement/intimacy, being a Role Model requires the brand not just to know but to seem to empower the customer.

Starbucks is an interesting case of a brand that has cycled through a number of phases in its Role Model relationship with customers. With its gourmet coffees, deliberate European feel and variously styled – but always casually comfortable – outlets, Starbucks fast became the state-of-the-art in coffee houses. Where else would you want to sit and linger over a coffee while occasionally tapping away at your iMac? However, as it became more and more ubiquitous – was there a city block in Manhattan in the year 2000 that did not have a branch? – and as other credible brands of coffee house started to appear, Starbucks lost its sheen.

Instead of new and charismatic, it started to seem old and neurotic. Though customers never lost their taste for the lattes and frappes, they complained constantly about the high prices and the length of time they had to wait for their order. They were certainly not getting any mentoring from the brand, and sales declined sharply in 2007. When Starbucks founder Howard Schultz once again took over the reins of management in 2008, he did two things; he closed a lot of outlets, part of his plan to restore the "distinctive Starbucks experience" by making it less ubiquitous, and he worked on the brand attitude.

In 2009, the company announced that it would be overhauling its menu and selling salads and baked goods without high-fructose corn syrup or artificial ingredients. In 2013, Starbucks began to post calorie counts on menus for drinks and pastries in all of their US stores. Arguably the brand's most "mentor-like" move was its announcement of its Starbucks College Achievement Plan, which offers financial assistance and personalized mentoring to all its employees to complete a bachelor's degree through Arizona State University's degree programs, delivered online. Although this is aimed at employees – of whom there are some 135,000 in the US – rather than customers, one of Schultz's stated aims is to encourage other companies to start similar programs for their employees. The brand attitude that that communicates will be clear to all.

4. Self-Differentiation

For many years, brand differentiation was regarded as being the main engine of brand growth, profitability, and brand value. Brands that were differentiated in consumers' eyes were successful; brands that failed to differentiate themselves did not prosper, while brands that lost their differentiation lost power and leverage in the marketplace. All this was true – up to a point – but it was missing an important link which is, of course, the brand attitude that gives differentiation its motive power. That attitude is the one we have already referred to as "There for Me." It is certainly good for a brand to be seen as distinctive and unique – but not if that difference makes it seem distant or self-centered. The brand's difference must be seen as inclusive of the customer, who thereby feels distinctive and unique too. In Chapter 6, we saw what happened to Compaq – a brand of computer whose differentiation had brought it great success throughout the 1980s, and allowed it to maintain a premium over its competitors, including the IBM PC. But Compaq was aloof from the marketplace, and its products were sold only through independent distributors. Around 1990, when the "Intel inside" sticker on every brand of personal computer finally convinced everyone that the name on the outside of the computer did not matter so much, Compaq lost its differentiation – and its place in the market. There was nothing left to drive the brand, because its attitude was the antithesis of "There for Me."

The lack of a "There for Me" attitude is a common problem for differentiated brands in many categories – whether that differentiation is a technological one like Compaq's, a prestige-based differentiation like the American Express Card, or a style-based differentiation like Lean Cuisine. Differentiation without "There for Me" is too iconoclastic, and will always restrict the brand to an elite group of consumers. This may work in luxury or fashion-based categories, but it is never suitable for mass market brands.

5. Playful

The Playful relationship embodies the pleasure principle; not in the sense of indulging in overly hedonistic excess, but in the way that childhood ludic behavior (play) is imported into adult life, and appropriately transformed by normally healthy adults. The pleasure principle is the antithesis of duty or obligation; it is fun without cost. Brands that embody this principle are seen as fun, cool, easy, and relaxing; at the same time, they only want to give pleasure, without expecting anything in return. Hedonic consumption too, as described in Chapter 3, whereby consumption of the brand evokes strong memories or emotions, can be a very important factor in this relationship; the memories, in this case, are of course always pleasurable.

Unlike other brand relationships – Reinforcement and Identification in particular – Playful is a relationship that can easily develop even when the consumer is not a regular user of the brand; neither component of this relationship – consumers' perceptions of the brand being fun and cool nor projections of the brand only wanting to give pleasure – depends on using the brand in order to be assimilated by the potential consumer. In fact, a Playful relationship is one of the most important precursors to and motivators for entering a brand's franchise and becoming a regular user.

Naturally, brands in leisure and entertainment categories can most easily develop a Playful relationship. Retail brands, in general, are more likely to build a Playful relationship with consumers; the well-known "therapeutic" value of shopping works precisely because of the pleasure principle, which channels an escape from or counterbalance to the obligations and duties of life. But brands in other types of category can also develop relationships with consumers on the basis of Play; we saw in Chapter 3 how luxuriously foamy bath soaps or imaginatively scented hair shampoos, which focus on the pleasures of using them rather than promising end results, are adopting the pleasure principle.

One important qualification for the successful development of a Playful consumer brand relationship is the issue of price. Price can represent not just the pecuniary cost of using a brand, but also a psychological cost. It depends very much on the consumer's relationship with money – their actual economic circumstances and psychological state; but developing a strong Playful relationship is usually harder for premium brands. The higher price means a higher psychological cost, which of course undermines the pleasure principle.

In order to illustrate these brand relationships, and how they work both within and between product categories, a brand relationship map for each one is shown on the following pages: Each brand relationship map plots the same set of brands on the two axes of the map – consumer perceptions on the horizontal axis, and brand attitudes on the vertical axis.

In each of seven very different product categories – including the somewhat whimsical "category" of Presidential Candidates (there were only two "brands" in this category at the time) – I have chosen one brand as an exemplar, a "banner" brand that generally leads its category. In addition to comparing these category-leading brands with each other, they are compared to the average of brands within their own category. With the exception of Presidential Candidates, all the categories are represented by from five to seven brands. From these maps we can learn a number of things:

1. To what extent a category-leading brand can step outside of the norms of its category, with regard to brand relationships, and to what extent it brings its category "baggage" with it when we compare it to leading brands of other categories. This is what I refer to as the "category effect," meaning that the brand in question appears strong in relation to brands in other categories, only because of its product category. In order to highlight category effects, the banner brand and its category average have been circled when they occupy similar positions on the brand relationship map.
2. On which of the Universal Brand Relationships each brand excels. Is the strength of its brand relationships inherent in the brand or in its product category?
3. Where "banner" brands have a strong relationship, what plays the larger role – perceptions of the brand or its attitudes? Which of the two is more critical to weaknesses in its relationships?

In all of the brand relationship maps that follow, the scales measuring brand perceptions on the horizontal axis and brand attitudes have all been standardized (to zero mean unit standard deviation) in order that they can be compared with each other.

Reinforcement – Exemplar, J&J

With the exception of Haircare and Presidential Candidates, there is no very marked category effect on this relationship. Amazon (etail) and Walmart (mass market retail) both outstrip their categories, but Johnson & Johnson is the Reinforcement brand par excellence – it is equally strong on both dimensions of the relationship; because J&J products perform well, they make the consumers

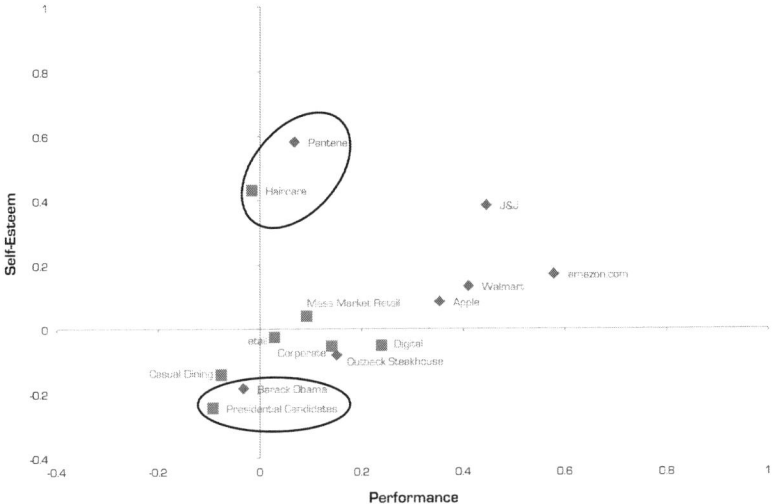

FIGURE 7.1 Universal Brand Relationships – Reinforcement

feel good about themselves; and because they feel good, they know that the brand performs well.

Digital brands as a category generally deliver performance, but that performance is not reinforced by a strong "good job" brand attitude. Using brands such as Google, Facebook, YouTube, and LinkedIn – the other brands in this category – evidently does not boost the self-esteem of the user. Why would that be the case? Each of these brands in its way has a unique functionality, so using them involves no actual brand choice as such; if you want to watch a clip from an old movie, where else other than YouTube can you find it? If you want to inform everyone you know instantly about some important development in your life, how else but via Facebook? The point is that enhanced self-esteem comes from having made a good *choice*; if you didn't have to make a choice – because there was no choice – you don't get the kudos. This is why Apple distances itself somewhat from the other digital brands. Apple is not unique in its basic functionality; there are other brands of computer, other smart phones and other tablets. You can get the self-awarded "smart" choice points by choosing Apple.

In contraposition to Amazon and Walmart, Pantene and its fellow haircare brands are strong on just the brand attitudinal component of this relationship – making the consumer feel good about her/himself and looking good to others. As discussed in Chapter 3, this reveals the true motivation for using a brand that focuses on "end results"; not because the user really expects a magical transformation; they expect and get "good enough" performance reinforced with the psychological reassurance about a job well done.

Identification – Exemplars, Walmart and Amazon

For this relationship four of the brands out-distance their categories; for J&J (corporate) and Outback Steakhouse (casual dining), it is old-fashioned brand love that makes the difference. Walmart and Amazon are not only loved more by the customer but also love the customer more; it is the superior ability of these brands to help consumers be themselves and express themselves that makes them stand out from both other brands in their categories and in general. The projection by the consumer that these two brands enable their self-expression is, as discussed earlier in this chapter, at least partially an *outcome* of feeling the brands' love; what contributes to that feeling of love from the brand is the projection that Walmart and Amazon are "There for *Me*."

Johnson & Johnson is also a very "There for Me" brand (see the Self-Differentiation map below); why does that not make it as loving a brand as Walmart or Amazon? Although J&J owns brands with relationships of their own – Tylenol, Listerine, and Band-Aid, etc. – the corporate brand's relationship equity undoubtedly derives from the products and sub-brands that bear just its own name; the J&J brand therefore essentially offers its own products to the consumer. Walmart and Amazon, on the other hand, do that and – in addition – they also offer the consumer a *choice of brands*. A choice of different brands is what makes consumers feel that Walmart and Amazon are helping them express themselves, and they therefore experience an additional dimension of the facilitating brands' love for them. So, although being "There for Me" is a necessary attitude for a loving brand – it is not sufficient.

Offering a choice of brands is obviously a unique characteristic of retail brands like Walmart and Amazon; but, as we can see from the positions on the

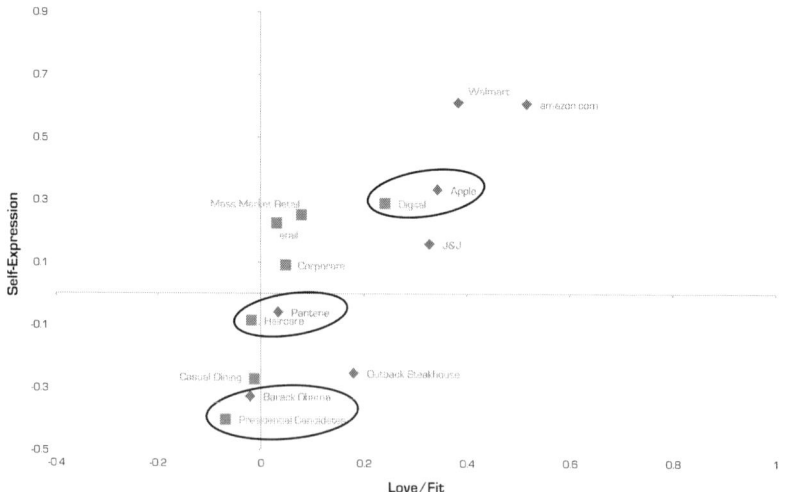

FIGURE 7.2 Universal Brand Relationships – Identification

map of the mass market retail and etail brand categories, that alone is not sufficient to facilitate the feeling of self-expression, which also depends on the brand being "There for Me." The two brand attitudes – self-expression facilitated by offering choices and being "There for Me" – work symbiotically to build the projection of the brand's love for the consumer.

I referred in Chapter 6 to the "epiphany" that I experienced when I was working with the old AT&T brand, the long-distance phone company; that competition is an essential precondition for brand loyalty; that the process of building loyalty to a brand comes about as a result of the consumer being able to make choices. We see here how the connection between brand choice and brand loyalty is mediated by these two important brand relationships – both of which are strongly associated with brand loyalty. Brand choice, in the case of Reinforcement, gives consumers permission to congratulate themselves on their own smarts, and empowers consumers' own freedom for self-expression in the case of Identification; brand choice is fundamental to both brand relationships.

Role Model – Exemplar, Apple

Here only two brands stand out – in general and in relation to their categories – Amazon and Apple. Both brands are highly charismatic leaders, progressive, technically advanced; more than that, they lead not just for the sake of leadership, but in order to inspire their users to aspire to those same qualities; they are role models.

Ironically, only one other brand/category has the same mentoring attitudes – Presidential Candidates; they aspire to fill the Role Model relationship – to inspire, to teach, to express common values, but these "brands" sadly lack the leadership qualities and charisma necessary to pull it off.

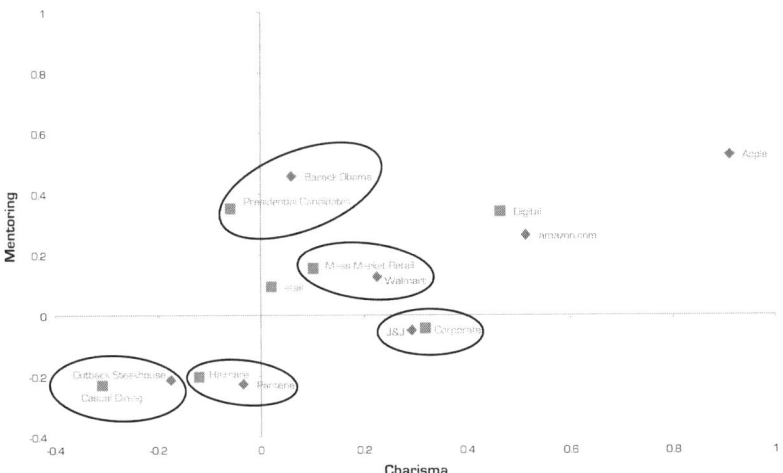

FIGURE 7.3 Universal Brand Relationships – Role Model

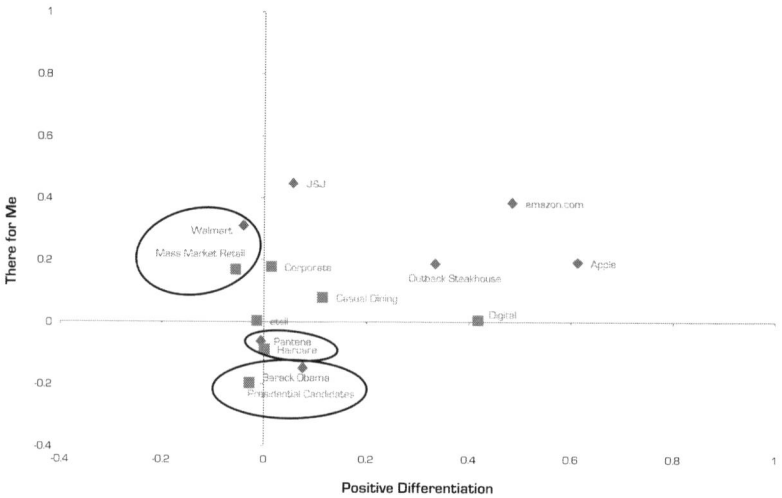

FIGURE 7.4 Universal Brand Relationships – Self-Differentiation

Self-Differentiation – Exemplars, Amazon and Apple

J&J's brand attitude is distinguished – in relation to other corporate brands and in general – as a brand that most has consumers' interests at heart, that responds to their needs, and tries to earn their loyalty; however, J&J is not otherwise more differentiated than other corporate brands. Amazon has the same level of "There for Me" attitudes, but is highly differentiated. Apple is even more differentiated than Amazon but the brand attitude is less strong.

These three brands stake out different points in the relationship space of Self-Differentiation, each with a different balance in the relative strengths of consumer perceptions and projections of brand attitude. Although Amazon and Apple probably have a more optimal balance than J&J, it is not possible a priori to judge between those of the two former brands; that is the kind of judgment that can only be made empirically, and is a topic which will be taken up in a later section of this chapter.

Playful – Exemplar, Amazon

The category effect on this relationship is quite strong; casual dining and digital brands – and to a lesser extent mass market retail brands too – are seen as cool, fun, friendly, and stylish. Casual dining brands, in addition, excite and evoke memories of good things; they are not just fun, but they also give pleasure.

The one brand that stands out from its category and all the other brands except Outback Steakhouse is Amazon; this brand embodies play – pure fun, the absence of "duty," indulgence without consequences – more than any other. Outback Steakhouse, on the other hand, is just the strongest brand in a category that represents the pleasure principle.

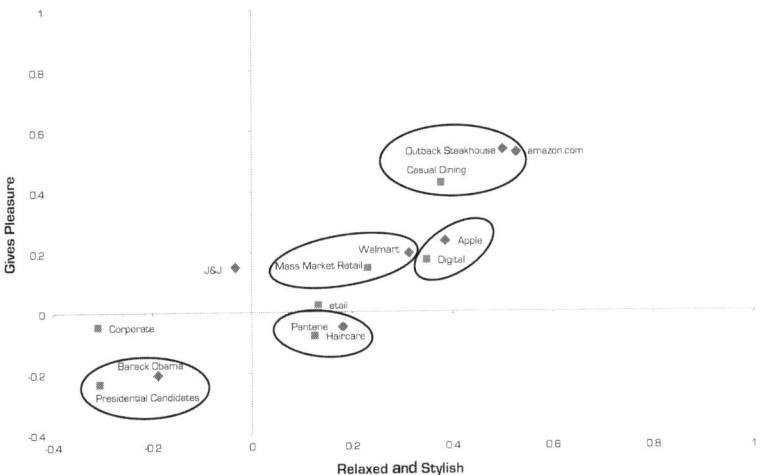

FIGURE 7.5 Universal Brand Relationships – Playful

Balancing Brand Perceptions and Brands' Attitudes

Up to this point in the description of the five universal brand relationships, other than emphasizing the importance of the two components of each and the synergies between them, I have remained neutral as to which of the two – consumers' perceptions of the brand or their projections of its attitude – is the more important. This begs the question of whether brand management should – or could – advance one without managing the other; remember that in a world of unforeseen consequences all other things are rarely ever equal. Pushing prestige risks creating a distant and arrogant brand attitude unless it is managed; leveraging leadership qualities risks leaving the brand in splendid isolation, unless it overtly recognizes and encourages the leadership aspirations of its users too; 1980s Maxwell House coffee became all brand attitude at the expense of substance; and so on. But in the reality of limited resources and marketing budgets, where should the priorities lie?

Unsurprisingly, there is not one simple answer to this question of which is more important. Different product categories require different emphases and within categories brands are different. However, by far the most important variable is the nature of the customer; specifically, at what point are they on the brand usership/loyalty "funnel?" I use the term funnel to describe the normal objectives of marketing activity; to attract and gather as many people as possible toward the brand, to convince a high proportion of them to try or buy the brand, and to maximize the proportion of the brand's buyers or users who will buy it again, use it regularly, and prefer it to other brands in its category. At each of these stages, consumers' relationships with a brand can vary in terms of which of the two components is more influential in propelling them further along the funnel. In order to see how this works, we shall be looking again at relationship maps for each of the five universals but, instead of plotting specific brands, the maps show the average position of all brands' relationships at six stages on the funnel:

- non-users who have a negative interest in purchasing the brand in the future; these would include people who are hardly aware that the brand exists as well as those who have used the brand in the past, but no longer do so
- non-users who are neither negative nor positive about purchasing the brand
- non-users who have a positive interest in purchasing the brand in the future
- occasional and infrequent users of the brand
- regular users of a brand who describe it as one of several brands they purchase in the category
- regular users who describe the brand as the one they prefer to buy.

For Reinforcement, the principal direction of movement at early stages of the funnel is vertical, i.e. in the direction of stronger brand attitude. Although there are some small improvements in the expected performance of the brand, it is principally the anticipated boost to self-esteem that makes non-users more interested in using or buying it. Once over the threshold and using the brand occasionally, it is then that increased satisfaction with performance that takes over and propels the consumer up the funnel toward more regular use and brand preference. Moral – to attract new users into a brand's franchise don't just tell them how good the brand is; let them see how much better *they* will be. After that, of course, the brand does have to deliver satisfactorily.

This lesson has long been internalized by marketing and advertising people as "sell consumer end benefits, not product attributes." David Ogilvy used to say "people don't want 3/8 inch drill bits, they want 3/8 inch holes." But

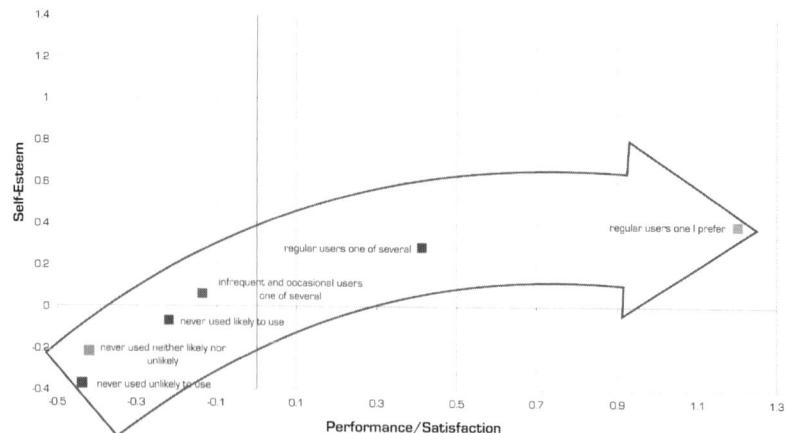

FIGURE 7.6 Brand Relationships and the Usership/Loyalty Funnel – Reinforcement

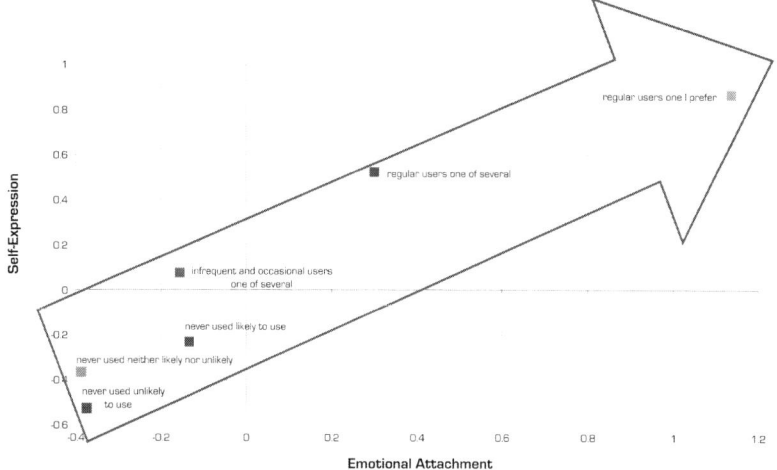

FIGURE 7.7   Brand Relationships and the Usership/Loyalty Funnel – Identification

that doesn't go far enough; what they actually want is the self-satisfaction and approval from others for having fixed the shelves well. Huggies diapers advertising always leads with images of happier babies, rather than with the superior water-tight technology of the diapers; a happy baby is certainly a lead indicator of most mothers' self-esteem.

With Identification, there are incremental improvements in both love for the brand and by the brand all the way up the funnel. As I have already shown in Chapter 1 and reiterated earlier in this chapter, the benefits of the brand being loved by the consumer only fully accrue when there is a matching emotional response to the consumer by the brand. Unlike Reinforcement, where the two

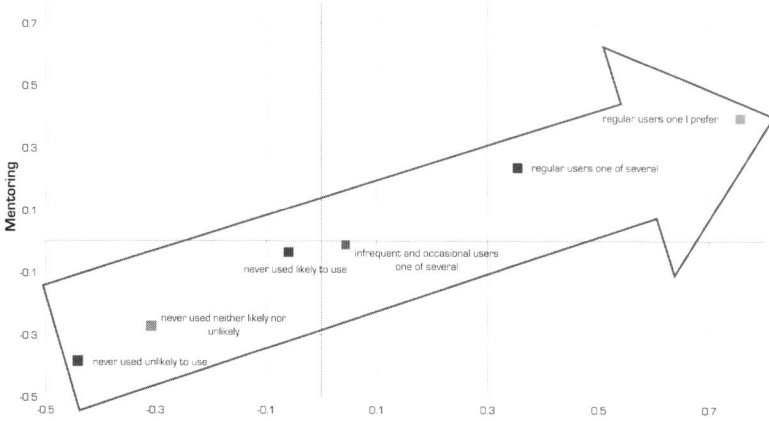

FIGURE 7.8   Brand Relationships and the Usership/Loyalty Funnel – Role Model

sides of the relationship play a complementary role at different points along the funnel, here they have to be in lock-step all the way.

In the Role Model relationship too, advancing along the funnel is associated with a simultaneous strengthening of both perceptions of brand charisma and mentoring. However, what is notable here is that every step up the funnel comes with a 50 percent greater increase of charisma than in the projection of brand mentoring; the slope of the line connecting the points of the funnel is much less steep than in the case of Identification, where the incremental changes are roughly equal. What does this mean?

There are two answers to this question; one is the statistical one, which says that there is less variance in mentoring than in charisma; if we were to use statistical regression to explain progress up the funnel in terms of the two relationship components, then mentoring would result as less influential than charisma. But regression is an additive model, and the relational model is not additive. The relational answer is that it takes relatively smaller improvements in mentoring than in perceptions of the brand's charisma in order to achieve a given improvement in the strength of a brand's franchise; both are necessary but – returning to the theoretical question, about where the priorities should lie – the return on the investment put into mentoring is higher than on that invested in building brand charisma.

For Self-Differentiation, the picture is the reverse of what we saw with reinforcement; increasing levels of non-user interest in brands are associated more with greater brand differentiation. Differentiation is an engine that can drive a brand in the early stages of its life; it can get people to the threshold of the brand's franchise. But unless that differentiation is personalized, experienced as

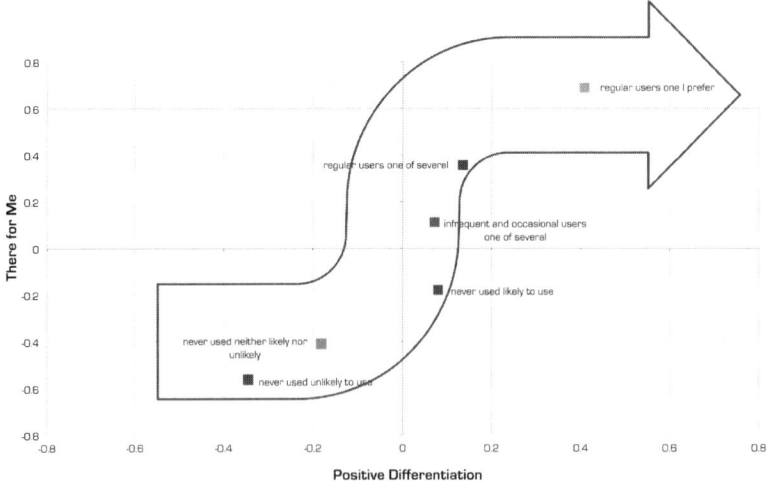

FIGURE 7.9 Brand Relationships and the Usership/Loyalty Funnel – Self-Differentiation

something that serves the interests and the ego of the consumer rather than of the brand, then the consumer will remain there on the threshold. The switch to a "vertical" movement up the funnel – from intending users to regular but not loyal users of brands – is quite dramatic. But Differentiation kicks in again at the apex of the funnel – the arrow should really be "S"-shaped; it is further Differentiation that secures users' preference and loyalty to the brand.

Across all points of the funnel, the variance in Differentiation is a third less than in "There for Me." So can we make the same ROI argument that we did for the Role Model relationship? Can we say that, if push comes to shove, focusing just on improving Differentiation will give a greater return on market-ing expenditures? The difference between this relationship and the Role Model one is that we are dealing with a curve rather than a straight line; at a certain point in the funnel, the return on greater Differentiation is virtually zero; the interested non-user does not cross the threshold and become a user unless the "There for Me" brand attitude becomes apparent. Without it, the brand will never reach that sunlit upland where it can again leverage Differentiation to build brand loyalty; it will – at best – remain a niche brand.

The Playful relationship shows a similar pattern to that of Identification; progress up the funnel is associated with equal and simultaneous improvements in both consumer perceptions and brand attitude. What is unique about this relationship is that most of the variance in both of its components is concen-trated at the lower end of the funnel – between brands unlikely to be used and brands infrequently used. The major influence of the Playful relationship is in arousing consumers' interest in a brand and getting them to try it. Once the consumer has entered the franchise, the brand must build other relationships in order to secure more regular use and brand preference.

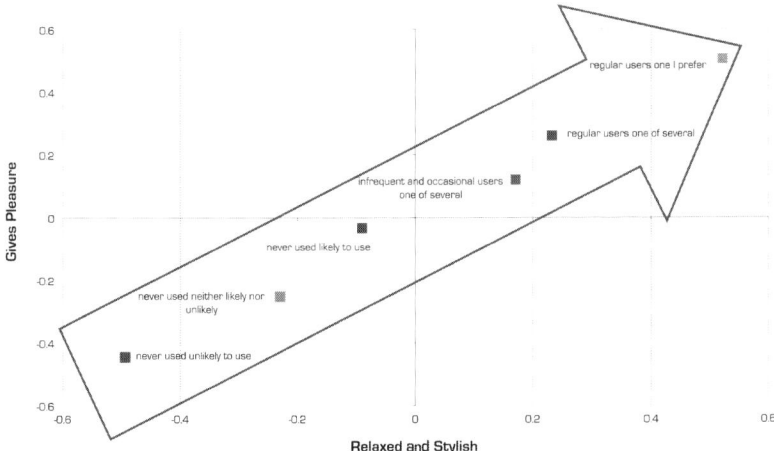

FIGURE 7.10 Brand Relationships and the Usership/Loyalty Funnel – Playful

A classic case of a successful Playful-based brand introduction that I am familiar with is that of Unilever's fabric softener brand, Snuggle. (In Italy, I was involved in the launch of the brand, known there as "Coccolino.") I have described this case fully in Chapter 3; suffice it to say that the key factor in engineering a pleasure-giving brand attitude from the outset was the lower price of the brand, compared to its competitors.

Another lesson to be taken from this connection between price and brand attitude is that a "price" brand already starts with the right attitude for forming a Playful relationship; what it needs to do is to ensure that the right consumer perceptions are in place too. A successful relationship strategy for maximizing the chances of building a franchise for a price brand is to make the brand fun, relaxing, and stylish. It is important to reiterate that this is a relationship strategy for brand-building, not brand salvaging; it is unlikely to help former full-price brands that are considering a price strategy in order to retain users.

Brand Relationship Erosion

Before finishing this description of the universal brand relationships, there is one last issue to be considered. In the last section, I showed the roles that these relationships play as consumers develop ever-closer involvement with brands; what happens as people move in the opposite direction, as they become disenchanted, disappointed, or just bored with a brand? To answer this, we cannot just follow the arrows of the funnel back in the opposite direction; relationship development and relationship decline are not symmetrical.

In order to plot this negative trajectory, we can consider the difference between users of a brand – infrequent, frequent, loyal or not – and reluctant users, those who say that they only use it when they have no other choice. We can move even further in this direction by comparing reluctant users to ex-users. The relationship change that accompanies this distancing from the brand is first and foremost a loss of Identification; the brand is both less loved and loves less. Consumers rationalize this loss of identification in terms of their being less satisfied with its performance; they also lose the feeling that the brand is "There for Me," and the brand loses its charismatic power to attract them. It is almost literally a process of falling out of love.

What then are the implications for protecting a brand from this process? People will generally go on loving a brand if it demonstrates its love for them. The most effective bulwarks against brand distancing are thus the two brand attitudes instrumental in creating the feeling of a brand's love; facilitating the consumer's autonomy and need for self-expression and demonstrating that everything the brand does is for the benefit of and in the interest of the consumer.

The purpose of this last section has been to contrast the roles of consumers' perceptions and brands' attitudes at different points in the development of a brand's franchise. What it has demonstrated is the close connection between the strength of a brand's relationships and the health of its franchise – the number of its regular purchasers, the frequency with which they buy or use it, and how loyal they are to it. Certain specific connections have also emerged – for example, how developing a Playful relationship with non-users of a brand can arouse interest in trial, or how Identification with the brand represents best assurance of sustained brand loyalty. The next stage in this exposition of a general model of Consumer Brand Relationships is to move from the anecdotal to a more formal model. That is the topic of the next – and final – chapter.

8

BRAND RELATIONSHIPS AND THE VALUE OF BRANDED BUSINESSES

In the previous chapter I described the characteristics of five universal brand relationships, which are essentially product category neutral, and which hence provide a more generalized framework for understanding and managing consumer brand relationships. I also began to explore quantitatively how these universal brand relationships influence consumers' behavior. In this chapter, I am going a step further by defining and testing a formal statistical model, the principal objective of which is to measure the influence of consumer brand relationships on the size and strength of brand franchises, and ultimately on the value of branded businesses, as reflected in their stock market valuations.

In its general objective, this model is no different from other models that connect the micro-level activities of brand management with macro-level market phenomena. The utility of such models lies in providing, for marketing and senior corporate management, an objective measure of the impact, at the corporate level, of past marketing activities and expenditures, as well as a prescriptive formula for evaluating and guiding future brand strategies, designed to maximize shareholder value.

The model described in this chapter is constructed in two parts, which I will refer to as the "micro" model and the "macro" model.

The micro model is designed to quantify the influence of each of the universal brand relationships on the size and strength of brands' consumer franchises. It is illustrated conceptually in Figure 8.1.

The macro model, illustrated in Figure 8.2, measures the influence on the financial market valuation of a branded business of two variables derived from the micro model:

- the size and strength of the brand's customer franchise, and
- the equity created by the brand's relationships with consumers.

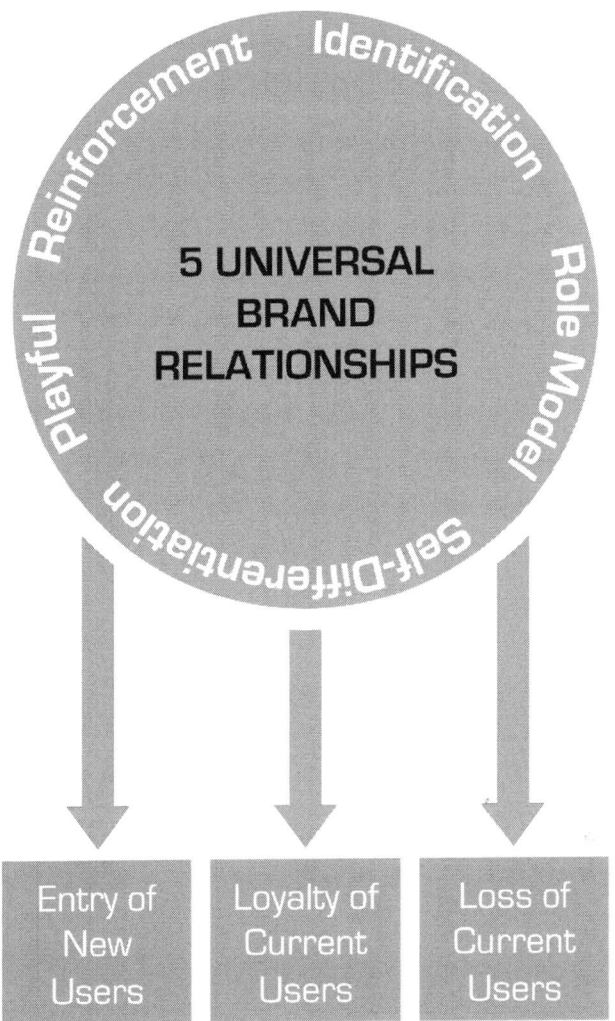

FIGURE 8.1 Micro Model

If this sounds like a "double-dip" for brand relationships, it is: They influence market valuations of branded businesses both directly and indirectly, via their influence on brands' customer franchise development. This is not, however, a double-counting, because the two points of influence of brand relationships occur in different time periods: If their direct influence on brand value is measured in time t, the current accounting period say, then their influence on brand franchise occurs in previous accounting periods; t-1, t-2, etc. The model operationalized and described here is not however a time-series model; it is based on cross-sectional measurement at one point in time, and

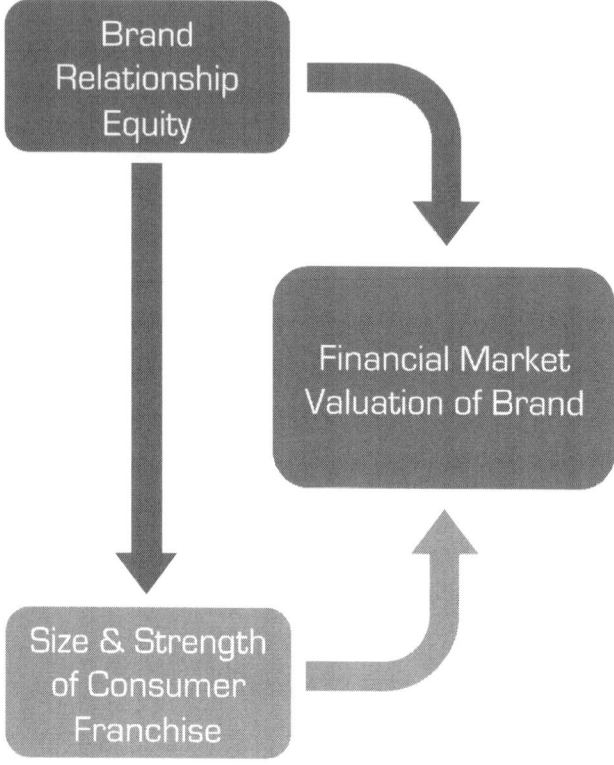

FIGURE 8.2 Macro Model

therefore has to include the double influence of brand relationships collapsed into a single time period.[1]

This type of model is known technically as an "aggregate flow" model, a statistical regression-based model that is broken down into a series of sequential flows or processes. This gives it a greater diagnostic capability than one big statistical "black box," a single regression equation that connects all the inputs with the output. The whole model, indicating the connections between the micro and macro sub-models, is shown in Figure 8.3.

At a more detailed level, the model consists of the following regression equations:

Micro Model

1.1 Expanding the Brand Franchise – attracting new users: This equation estimates the influence of each of the five universal brand relationships on non-users' interest in purchasing a brand.

1.2 Strengthening the Brand Franchise – building brand preference: In this equation, the influence of each of the brand relationships on users' attachment to a brand is estimated.

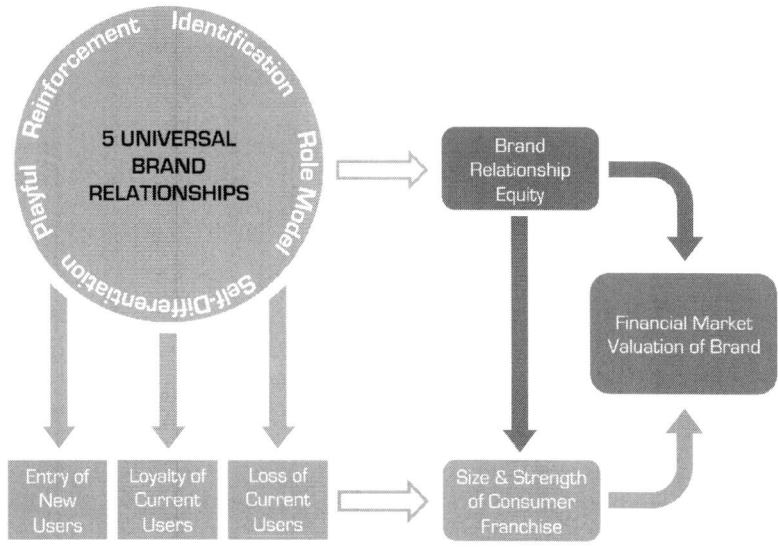

FIGURE 8.3 Micro Model/Macro Model

Macro Model

2.1 The first function of the macro model is a regression equation connecting overall Franchise Strength (a measure of which will be defined later) with overall measures of brand relationship – summary measures reflecting the relative importance of the five individual relationships, as determined by the micro model equations.

2.2 The second function of the model is the one connecting the financial value of brands, as reflected in their stock price, with Brand Relationships and overall Franchise Strength.

Model Operationalization

A. Defining the Model's Parameters

One of the most challenging problems in operationalizing this model was devising a statistic – or a set of statistics – to represent the quantitative value of brand relationships. Throughout this book I have emphasized the qualitative difference between the two relational components – consumers' perceptions and their projections of brands' attitudes – and the fact that these cannot simply be added together to measure the strength of the relationship. So what are the alternatives? Multiplication, quadratic combination, logarithmic transformations? Any one of these may be appropriate, but they are all theoretical and arbitrary. I could have experimented with all of these until I got "the right answer"; but, no less important than fitting a model that proves my overall hypothesis – that brand relationships influence the stock price of branded businesses – is the need to articulate and validate reasonable hypotheses for each of the individual processes that mediate it. So, for the same reason that the model is specified in terms of a series of explicit processes, I have tried to avoid using opaque statistical devices in order to get from A to B; the model hopefully has *process validity* as well as output validity. In order to achieve that, it was necessary to take an empirical approach to "scoring" brand relationships, rather than an aprioristic one.

For each of the five brand relationships, the map space defined by the two components was partitioned into a number of sectors – each sector representing a different combination of values of the two relationship components. The database used is of a sufficient size that each sector is populated by a large number of brand observations, and can be compared to other sectors in terms of a number of different criteria; for example, what percentage of brands in a sector are used? How frequently? What percentage of the non-used brands are actively under consideration for purchase?

The results of this exercise were a vindication of the decision to maintain a non-additive methodology for calculating relationship scores. If we imagine one of these behavioral criteria – for example, the percentage of users or the proportion of loyal users within each sector of a relationship map – as a third, vertical dimension of the map, the resulting "behavioral response" surfaces are nothing like the mono-tonically slanting plane that an additive model would have created. The surfaces are often extensively "curved," and in many cases there are concave folds in the surface, indicating sectors where an increase in one of the relationship components, without a corresponding increase in the other, actually results in a weakening of the relationship. A simplified version of one of these 3D graphs, using actual data of the Self-Differentiation relationship, is shown in Figure 8.4. It illustrates quite dramatically how pushing brand imagery – in this case Differentiation – without a corresponding improvement in brands' attitude – There for You – can prove to be either non-productive or even counter-productive.

At the lowest level of Brands' Attitude (line A–B) the behavioral response to increased brand image is initially positive, but peaks at mid levels of image; as brand image increases beyond this point, the behavioral response becomes negative.

At middle levels of Brands' Attitude (line C–D), the behavioral response is initially commensurate with the improvement in brand image. However, beyond a mid level of brand image, the behavioral response flattens.

Only at the higher levels of Brands' Attitudes (line E–F) does the behavioral response continuously increase as brand image improves.

Two behavioral criteria[2] were selected to determine the brand relationship score for each sector of the brand relationship map:

- for brands *used*, a statistic based on the average strength of preference in each sector of the brand relationship map
- for brands *not used*, a measure of the average level of purchase interest in each sector.

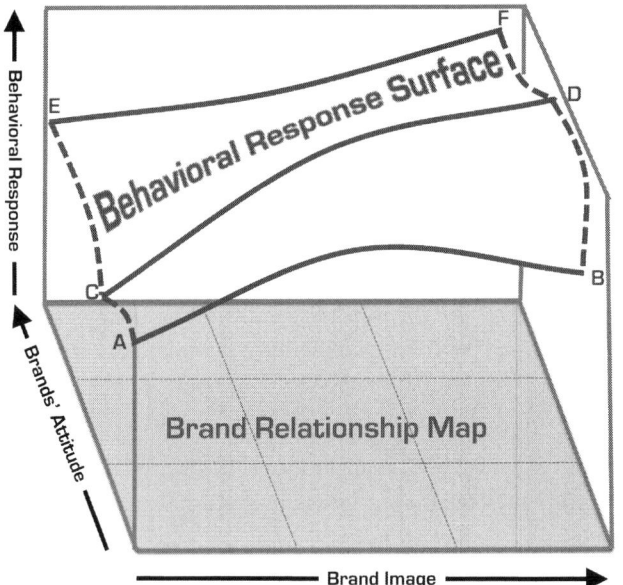

FIGURE 8.4 Behavioral Response Surface

For each specific brand, its average relationship score thus depends on its distribution across the different sectors of the map, and the scoring of each of those sectors. Each brand also has two scores for each relationship – one derived from its users and one from its non-users.

B. Estimating the Micro Model

The first stage in model construction was to estimate the influence of individual brand relationships on the formation, growth, and maintenance of brand franchises, something that was done informally in the previous chapter. This involved two sets of linear regressions.

1.1 Expanding the brand franchise – attracting new users

This equation estimates the influence of each of the five universal brand relationships on non-users' interest in purchasing a brand. The dependent variable is non-users' purchase interest, measured on a five-point scale from "very unlikely to purchase" to "very likely to purchase"; the independent variables are the non-users' relationship scores for each of the five, the calculation of which was described above.

The regression is statistically significant, with an explained variance (R^2) of 21 percent. Each of the five universal relationships makes a statistically significant contribution to the explanation of the dependent variable, in descending order of standardized regression coefficients, as shown in Table 8.1:

TABLE 8.1 Standardized Regression Coefficients: Regression of Non-Users' Likelihood of Purchasing on Brand Relationships

Playful	0.16
Self-Differentiation	0.15
Reinforcement	0.14
Identification	0.12
Role Model	0.12

As presaged informally in the previous chapter, Playful and Self-Differentiation are two brand relationships that can easily develop before the consumer has experience of purchasing or using a brand, and are important stages in the development of a consumer's involvement with a brand prior to purchase.

1.2 Strengthening the brand franchise – building brand preference

In this equation, the influence of each of the brand relationships on users' attachment to a brand is estimated. The dependent variable is a three-point scale, articulated as follows:

- a brand I would only use if there was no other alternative
- one of several brands that I use
- the one brand I prefer to use.

The independent variables in this case are the users' relationship scores for each of the five brand relationships.

This regression too is statistically significant, with an explained variance (R^2) of 20 percent. In this case, however, only four of the relationships contribute significantly; in descending order of standardized regression coefficients, they are shown in Table 8.2:

TABLE 8.2 Standardized Regression Coefficients: Regression of Users' Strength of Preference on Brand Relationships

Identification	0.22
Reinforcement	0.19
Self-Differentiation	0.07
Role Model	0.07

This is almost exactly the reverse of their order in influencing non-users' purchase intentions (Table 8.1), and in fact Playful – the most influential relationship in that regression – here has no influence on building users' brand preference. Again, this was something that we had already seen informally in the previous chapter.

C. From Micro to Macro

Building an aggregate flow model requires the definition of the parameters at varying levels of specificity or generality. In the micro model, two specific behavioral

TABLE 8.3 Weights Used in Computing Brand Relationship Equity Indices

	Non-Users	Users
Reinforcement	0.20	0.39
Identification	0.13	0.46
Role Model	0.16	0.08
Self-Differentiation	0.22	0.07
Playful	0.29	0.00

processes were modeled – franchise expansion and franchise strength – within the first function of the overall model. For the macro model, we now move up an order of generalization; from specific brand franchise processes to overall brand franchise strength, and from individual brand relationships to overall brand relationship strength. For this purpose, we need two new metrics; *Brand Relationship Equity (BRE)* and *Dynamic Franchise Strength*.

The *BRE* is based on the regressions in the micro model; the measure is computed as a weighted average of the five individual brand relationship scores, where the weights are derived from the partial correlation coefficients in the two regressions of the micro model. The estimating procedure was done separately for users and non-users of brands, resulting in two BRE statistics; Table 8.3 shows the relative weights that each of the five Universal Relationships had in computing the summary statistic for each.

It is possible to combine the two statistics into one aggregate Brand Relationship Equity statistic for each brand, which reflects both the weighted influence of each of the five brand relationships and the relative proportions of users and non-users of the brand. The bigger the brand franchise, the more the aggregate BRE reflects the strength of the Reinforcement and Identification relationships; the smaller the brand franchise, the more the aggregate BRE reflects its strengths on the other relationships. Although this aggregate statistic has its uses, for the purpose of the model I have maintained the two separate BREs, as this preserves a greater diagnostic capability.

The *Dynamic Franchise Strength* metric incorporates all of the dynamic processes that create the ongoing size and strength of a brand's franchise:

- the number of people using the brand on a regular or occasional basis
- the level of commitment of users to the brand
- the number of new users entering the franchise
- the number of users likely to exit the franchise.

Why would I include the influence of not-yet users and not-yet non-users in a metric representing brand franchise? As mentioned above, I am trying to capture with cross-sectional data the dynamic aspects of a brand's franchise; some of today's non-users will be users tomorrow; equally, some of today's users will not be users tomorrow. My ultimate aim is to connect consumers'

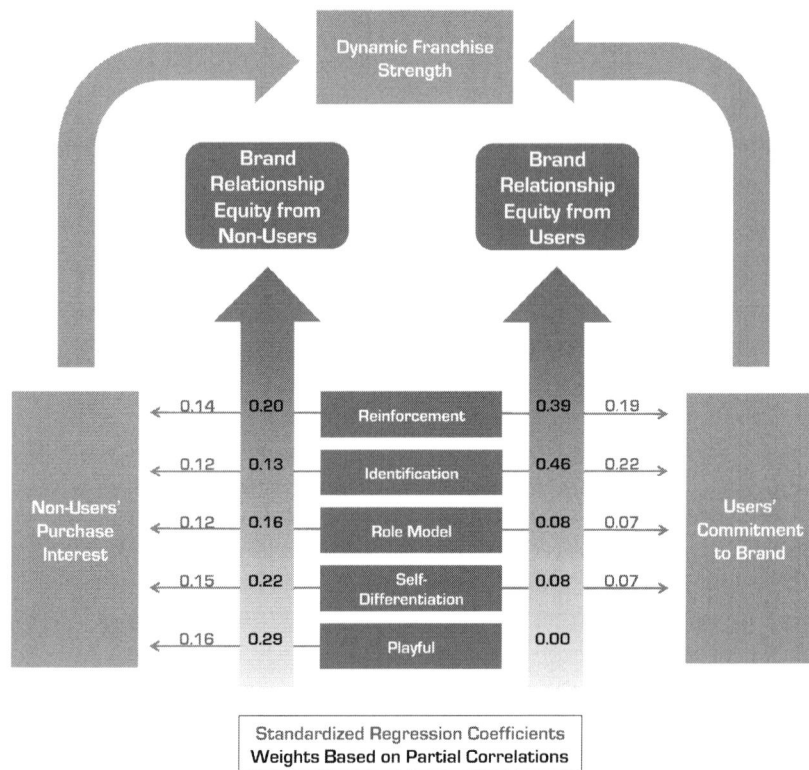

FIGURE 8.5 Estimated Micro Model

brand relationships to the financial value of branded businesses, which are certainly based on expectations about the future as well as on past and current performance. It is therefore important to try and reach beyond the static picture in time that our cross-sectional data provides.

Figure 8.5 summarizes the point we have reached in the process of building the model.

The chart shows the parameters of the micro model, the influence of individual brand relationships on specific behavioral processes that determine the size and strength of brands' consumer franchises. It also illustrates (with the block arrows) the construction of the "macro" level metrics for the next stage of modeling.

D. Estimating the Macro Model

The macro model estimates the overall influence of Brand Relationships on the size and strength of brand franchises.

2.1   The first function of the macro model is a regression equation connecting these two statistics. The standardized regression coefficients of Dynamic Franchise Strength on the two BRE statistics are 0.72 for users and 0.23 for non-users; the R^2 is 53 percent. The influence of users' brand relationships is thus three times as great as the influence of non-users' brand relationships.

2.2   The second function of the model is the one connecting the financial value of brands, as reflected in their stock price, with Brand Relationships and Dynamic Franchise Strength.

Clearly, not all brands have a publicly available financial value; most brands form part of a corporate portfolio, and the value of any one of these is not readily extractable from that of the financial value of the corporate owner. I therefore deliberately chose for my model a number of "mono-brands," brands which to all intents and purposes are co-identical with their corporate owner, and therefore whose financial value is available from published accounts. Among the 30 mono-brands in my database are Apple, Google, Facebook, Johnson & Johnson, Walmart, Amazon, American Express, Home Depot, BP, and GE.

The financial data that I took into consideration for the model included:

- Market Value (MV)
- Sales (S)
- Operating Profit (OP).

I found that for the 30 mono-brands these statistics are highly inter-correlated; "big" brands, brands with a high sales volume, tend to have a higher absolute Market Value and a higher Operating Profit. Brand size also creates a somewhat trivial correlation between the dollar values of these financial statistics and Brand Relationship values; big brands have more users and are more likely to be familiar to their non-users, both of which tend to inflate their Brand Relationship Equity values. It therefore made sense to try and remove the influence of brand size from the model. I "deflated" the financial statistics by investigating ratios such as Market Value to Sales, and Market Value to Operating Profit (p/e ratio). In order to correspondingly deflate the BRE values, I normalized them by the level of familiarity with the brand. My model, therefore, would be investigating the relationship between the strength of brands' relationships with consumers who are familiar with them and the ability of brands to convert a given level of sales or profits into stock market value.

The estimated influence of Brand Relationships and Dynamic Franchise Strength on the Market Value to Sales ratio was as follows.

The standardized regression coefficient of MV/S on Dynamic Franchise Strength is 0.28 and on familiarity-normalized BRE for users is 0.55; the coefficient of BRE for non-users is not significant; the R^2 is 31 percent.

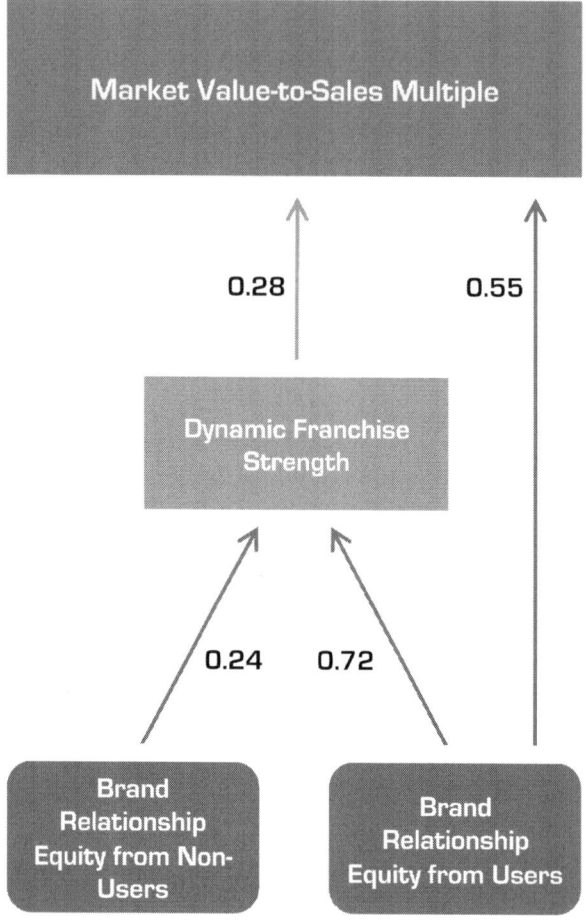

FIGURE 8.6 Estimated Macro Model (1)

Thus, independently of their significant influence in determining the size and strength of a brand's franchise, the strength of a brand's relationship with its users is twice as influential on the Sales-to-Market Value multiple as the size and strength of its franchise.

The first two functions of the macro model, with their parameter values, are summarized in Figure 8.6.

2.3 The third function of the macro model estimates the influence of Brand Relationships on the p/e (price to earnings) ratio of brands.

The standardized regression coefficient of p/e on BRE for users is 0.4 and for non-users is 0.34. The R^2 is 13 percent. This second function of the macro model is illustrated in Figure 8.7.

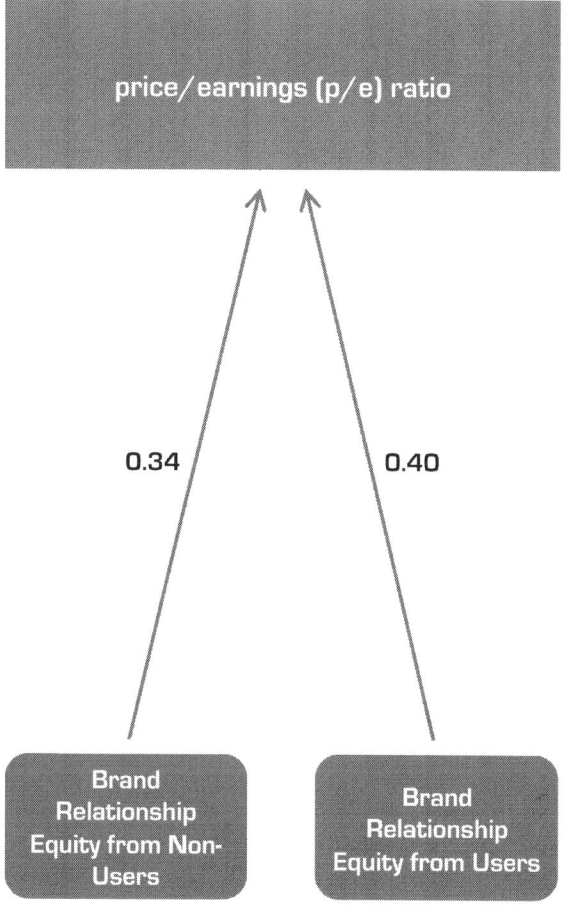

FIGURE 8.7   Estimated Macro Model (2)

Even though the explained variance is low, this significant regression compares interestingly with the previous one. Whereas a brand's ability to convert sales-to-market value depends directly only on the strength of *users'* brand relationships, the ability to convert earnings to share price depends directly also on the strength of *non-users'* brand relationships. In general, a high p/e suggests that investors are expecting higher earnings growth in the future – they are willing to pay more for a dollar of earnings now because they expect future earnings to be higher. Non-users' brand relationships are also future-oriented; they do not contribute to the current financial value of the brand except via their influence on the strength of the franchise, but they do have a direct influence on its expected future value. The significant influence of non-users' brand relationships on a ratio that reflects expected *future* value – in contrast to their lack of influence on current brand value – has a great deal of face validity.

Conclusions

I can now return to the question with which I opened the first chapter of this book: What makes a brand successful? In this chapter, I have defined success in a way that matters most to investors in a brand or in a company owning a portfolio of brands – its current and expected future financial value.

The current value of a brand depends partly on its sales volume – the size of its customer franchise, the level of purchasing activity of those customers, and their preference for buying that brand rather than one of its competitors. All this is highly dependent on the relationships the brand has with, primarily, its users, and secondarily with non-users. Current users are the main drivers of the franchise, but the ongoing health of the franchise is insured by non-users; they provide a reservoir of future users, which both keep the franchise growing and replace those who will drop out.

- The key relationships of users are Reinforcement and Identification. Strong Reinforcement results from good (or good enough) performance reinforced by the feeling of greater self-esteem that the brand gives the consumer. Strong identification results when the consumer not only loves the brand but feels loved by it too.
- For those not yet using the brand, the key relationships that attract them toward it are Playful (low cost/low risk enjoyment), Self-Differentiation (helping the consumer feel different), and Role Model (charismatic leadership combined with the feeling of being personally mentored).

Users' brand relationships play a second independent role in turning sales into market value. Strong Reinforcement and Identification act influentially on this multiplier.

The expected future value of the brand depends clearly on its earnings – how profitable it is now – but also on expectations about future earnings. The p/e ratio, which is an expression of the relationship between current earnings and future expectations, is highly dependent on the relationships that both users and non-users have with the brand.

The Future of the Relational Brand

A model should, of course, be predictive as well as descriptive; and, within the limits of its parameters, the model described here is capable of making predictions – not about what will happen, so much as what *could* happen. This type of model can be used to explore alternative "What if?" scenarios, a way for marketing and corporate management to make informed decisions about the future of their brands and branded businesses. However, to the extent that external influences on brand relationships that are not represented in the model change, then the model may need revising or re-estimating under those new circumstances.

As this model is based on the fundamentals of relationship psychology, it may be more robust than others; nonetheless, it is a reasonable hypothesis that the future of Consumer Brand Relationships will be different from the past because of the impact of the internet and social media in particular. Communications by brands have shifted radically toward the digital media, while communications by consumers – to and about brands – have acquired, via social media, a totally new channel that did not exist before. It is also undeniable that the future of Consumer Brand Relationships is in the hands of young people. It is via these two perspectives – the internet and young people – that I will briefly indulge in some crystal-ball gazing.

The Impact of the Internet and Social Media

I have repeatedly emphasized that the creation of brand relationships does not depend on the existence of any particular type of media – they are created in the consumer's mind, not in the media – but the expansion of digital forces and social media does certainly provide a new and powerful substrate for the formation and expression of consumer brand relationships. In particular, it is the consumer-to-consumer channel that social media has created which vastly expands the scope and influence of what we previously used to refer to as "word of mouth." To the extent that consumers use this channel to propagate their own perceptions of what brands are and what brands' attitudes are, and to the extent that other consumers are exposed to and influenced by others' perceptions, this can undoubtedly affect how readily brand relationships develop, and perhaps will also have an impact on the types of relationships that brands form.

I do not need to quote the changing media spend statistics in order to prove the fact that brand owners are shifting their communications to digital media; but the question one must ask is, from consumers' point of view, to what extent are their communications – from, to, and about brands – effectively shifting to digital media? In the following sections, I try to address this and other questions via analysis of the same 2012 multi-category study of brands that I have already quoted from in earlier chapters.

In the study consumers were asked where – in which media, including traditional television and print, as well as digital media – they had come into contact with each brand in the previous month. For 38 percent of the brands evaluated, consumers had had contact with them via the internet, and for just under a third of these brands the internet was the only form of contact with them.[3] Although media exposure is not a zero-sum game, if digital media are "taking over" from the traditional ones then it would be reasonable to expect to see some reduction in the latter for brands that the consumer interacts with on the internet. There is, in fact, a lower reporting of seeing TV advertising for these brands, but it is minimal – of the order of 10 percent – and there is much higher reporting – 50 percent and more – of print advertising than for brands not connected with on the internet. Allowing for all the limitations of ad hoc survey questions like this and the distortions produced by faulty recall, it does seem that *consumers who connect with brands on the internet are generally more involved with brand communications – both on and offline – than those who do not.* How do the relationships of brands connected with on the internet differ from those that are connected with only by traditional media?

Respondents in the study have been classified in terms of their predominant brand relationship – which of the five universal brand relationships gets the highest score – with each of the brands they evaluated. In those cases where the highest relationship score fell below a certain minimum,[4] the brand was classified as having "no strong relationships" with that respondent. This turned out to be the main difference between brands connected with on the internet and those connected with only by traditional media: The former brands were substantially less likely – of the order of 20 to 25 percent – to have "no strong relationships" than the latter; in terms of their predominant brand relationship, each of the five universals – with the exception of Playful[5] – benefited from this intensification of brand relationships as a consequence of internet contact. Not only was there a greater likelihood of brands connected via the internet having *any* significant relationship; *all* brand relationships were stronger for these brands. The Brand Relationship Map, Figure 8.8, shows the relative strengths of the five universal brand relationships for the averages of brands connected with via the internet and those connected with only via traditional media.[6]

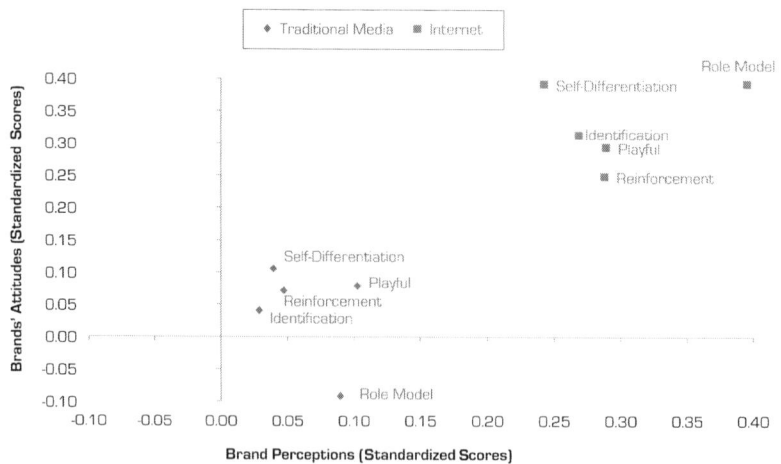

FIGURE 8.8 Brand Relationship Map – Brands Connected via Internet vs Only via Traditional Media

For all five of the brand relationships, brands connected via the internet have significantly stronger relationship scores than those connected only via traditional media. If this seems counter-intuitive, it is important to bear in mind the point I made earlier, that consumers who connect with brands on the internet are generally more involved with brand communications – both on and offline – than those who do not.

The question inevitably rises as to whether this is a real difference in the strength of brand relationships or whether it is a difference in the consumers with whom the brands have developed these relationships. The argument for the latter would be a latter-day version of the "selective migration" hypothesis; that consumers who are more "into" brands are the ones who have migrated to the internet for their brand communications. One way we might test this hypothesis is to look at the brand relationships that are mediated only via the internet and not at all via traditional media. The argument would be that these are the brand relationships of the avant-garde of the digital world; if their brand relationships are even stronger than the more mainstream internet users who also use traditional media, that is likely to be because of who they are rather than because of how they ingest brand communications. If that were the case – if it were consumers with inherently stronger brand relationships who were the first to embrace internet brand communications – then as more and more consumers start to connect with brands via the internet the stronger brand relationships we see now would become diluted by the inherently weaker brand relationships of the internet laggards, who are currently connecting with brands only via traditional media.

But that appears not to be the case; in terms of the distribution of predominant brand relationships, the internet only group is virtually indistinguishable from the internet plus traditional media group – if anything, they show a slightly higher percentage of "no strong relationships." Furthermore, as clearly shown by the Brand Relationship Map in Figure 8.9, all relationships are much stronger among the mixed media group than among the internet only group.

Again, if you are surprised by the relative weakness of brand relationships among the internet only group, bear in mind that consumers who only use digital media are below average users of media in general.

The picture we thus have is of an intensification – accelerated formation and strengthening – of brand relationships associated with exposure to a *mix* of internet and traditional media, compared to just the latter; while the complete exclusion of traditional media in favor of the internet shows a lower intensity of brand relationships compared to exposure to a mix of media. So the question becomes, is the current mixed media situation just a transitory state leading eventually to a complete shift from traditional media to the internet? If so, then the future of the relational brand looks considerably less rosy. I will resist the temptation to crystal gaze about this, as if I were a future trends pundit, and confine myself to the data at hand. We can get a limited glimpse into the future – "through a glass darkly,"

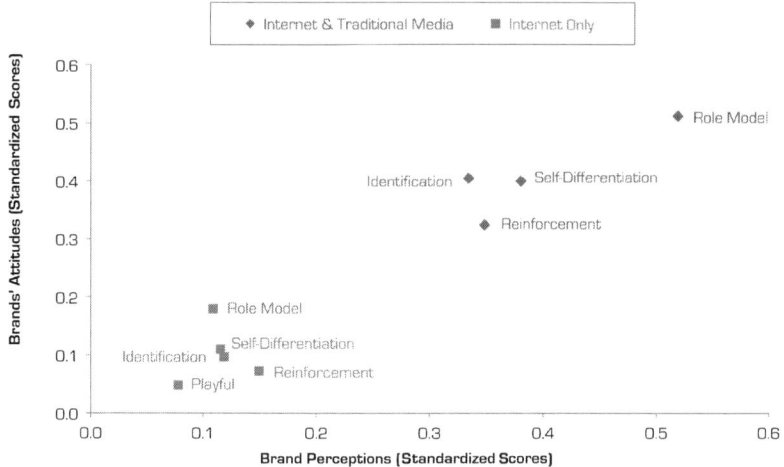

FIGURE 8.9   Brand Relationship Map – Brands Connected via Internet and Traditional Media vs Internet Only

as it were – by looking at the situation with regard to consumers' current age and generation cohorts.

Generational Change

The generational factor is, of course, not independent of the internet factor; so the first question I want to address is how the effects on brand relationships, which I have documented above, of different types of media exposure are likely to work out if age cohorts maintain their existing ways of interacting with brands. Figure 8.10 shows the situation.

The current situation (the "Total" bar in Figure 8.10) very much reflects that of the middle two age cohorts, 35 to 49-year-olds; a total of 38 percent of brands connect with consumers via the internet, of which 12 percent only via the internet. As we move into the millennial cohorts, under 34 years, there is an expansion of both total internet contact, to about 50 percent, and of internet only contact, to about 15 percent. So the news is both good in the short term – as the use of mixed traditional media and internet expands – and less good in the longer term, if the current pattern of the 18 to 24-year-olds starts to become dominant. But, before becoming too gloomy about the possible effects of changing media use, we will observe directly what the current brand relationships of millennial consumers promise for the future. Figure 8.11 shows the predominant brand relationships for age cohorts.

The first consistent pattern detectable, as we move across the age cohorts, is a slight decline of the "no strong relationships" classification among younger

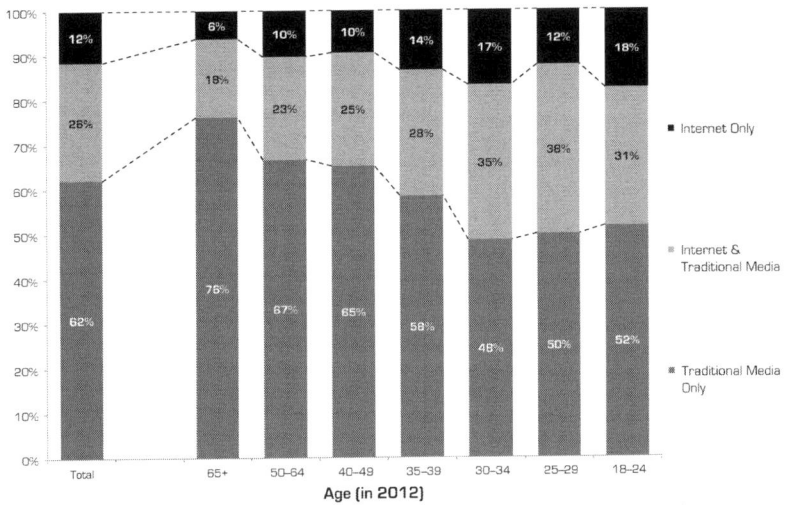

FIGURE 8.10 Type of Media Contact with Brands by Age Cohort

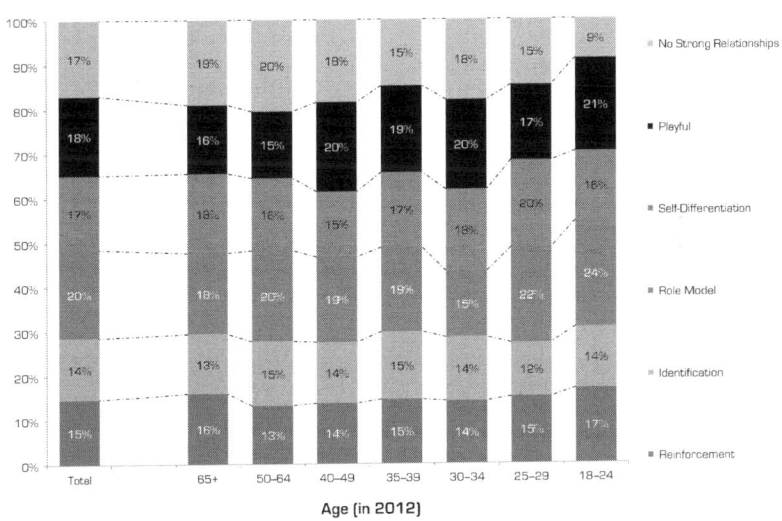

FIGURE 8.11 Predominant Brand Relationships by Age Cohort

millennials, particularly the 18 to 24-year-olds. In terms of specific brand relationships, the only consistent pattern across the age cohorts is a growth in the predominance of Role Model. So the process of brand relationship formation among millennials is at least as active as among other age cohorts; how strong are their brand relationships?

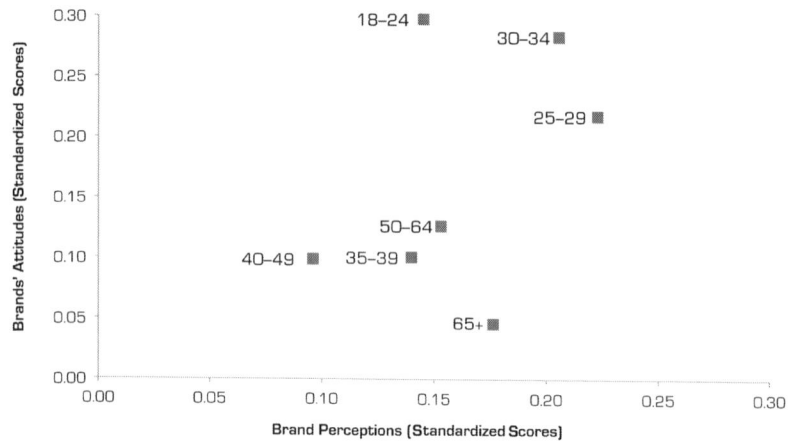

FIGURE 8.12 Brand Relationship Map – Averages of Five Universal Brand Relationships by Age Cohort

Figure 8.12 shows, for each age cohort, the average strength of brand perceptions and brands' attitudes across all five Universal Brand Relationships. (There are differences between the five universals, but these are less important than the average trend; and the chart needed in order to compare all five individually for each of the seven age cohorts is a horror story!) What leaps to the eye on this Brand Relationship Map is how *millennials' perceptions of brands' attitudes are so much stronger than the older age cohorts'*. The trend is not a continuous one: The 30 to 34 and 25 to 29 age groups are "reversed"; but perhaps that difference is too fine to observe. In contrast, there is no consistent trend in the strength of brand perceptions; the largest gap is less than half the size of the gap between the oldest and youngest age cohorts. Millennials' brand relationships are at least as strong as the older cohorts', but they are composed differently. It seems as if the future of the relational brand depends more so than ever on brands' attitudes.

Based on the evidence I have shown, here are some general conclusions that can be drawn about the future of brand relationships:

- The shift from traditional to digital media has accelerated or facilitated the formation of consumers' brand relationships.
- Although the overall complexion of consumers' brand relationships may change generally, as a result of the differential use of digital media between categories or between brands, for any given brand increased digital exposure will accelerate the formation of brand relationships and make them stronger.
- Although the complete eclipse of traditional media by digital media would not be beneficial for brand relationships, there is no evidence that that will occur in the short to medium term.

- Even though the youngest age cohort of millennials – those between 18 and 24 years of age in 2012 – are not surprisingly the ones most inclined toward an exclusively digital media world, their brand relationships are currently strong. The current brand relationships of millennials provide compelling evidence that the relational brand will depend more than ever on brands' attitudes in the future.

Because it consists of two distinct and mostly independent elements, the relational brand is a more complex construct than the brand that is conceptualized in other Consumer Brand Relationship models. The relational brand has intentionality, and so has attitudes in addition to its attributes; I don't believe that I "discovered" brands' attitudes; they have appeared for many years – perhaps under other guises – in advertising briefs, marketing communications strategies, and market research studies. What I think I have done is to individuate brands' attitudes as a category, and prove the importance of treating them as a distinct and quasi-independent aspect of consumers' perceptions; it is only this perspective that enables their purposive management. What I hope to have shown in this book is how important the management of brands' attitudes – as well as brand image – has been in the past and, by all indications, how much more so it is destined to be in the future.

Notes

1 In the regression analyses that are used to estimate the model, I have ensured that the regression estimates are not biased by this double use of brand relationship-derived measures as explanatory variables.

2 As these behavioral criteria are also used to define independent variables in the model, it was important to maintain independence between the scoring procedure and the statistical modeling. Accordingly, the development of the scoring was carried out using a randomly selected sample from the database; another similarly selected sample was held out for the purposes of developing the model.

3 In order to avoid proving the obvious, all internet brands – Facebook, Google, Amazon, etc. – were excluded from this analysis.

4 Equal to the lowest quartile of the distribution of relationship scores for all brands.

5 Casual dining brands – brands most likely to have a Playful relationship – are less likely than others to be contacted via the internet.

6 Brands with "no strong relationships" were excluded from both groups.

APPENDIX

Researching the Relational Brand

I was a market researcher before I became anything else, and it was through market research that I discovered the Relational Brand. As a researcher, my job was to propose research methodologies for obtaining different types of marketing information – including information about brands. Although probably most of the projects that I designed and worked on involved fairly standardized methodologies, every so often a need for information arose that required – at the very least – an adaptation to a standard methodology. Over time, I became increasingly aware of the limitations of standardized methodologies, and the desirability of keeping an open methodological mind in all cases. You can't "reinvent the wheel" for each new project; for much of my career, I was designing research projects to a price and scope at which they would be affordable, and also would hopefully show a profit at the end for the organization that employed me; but you can avoid automatically allocating every Request for a Proposal into a rigid template.

One of the most ironclad of methodological classifications is the distinction between qualitative and quantitative research. It tends to divide people – both research practitioners and users – and organizations. Advertising and product development people and start-up organizations love qualitative research, which almost always means focus group discussions, while governmental and public institutions and older, larger marketing companies will not make a move without quantitative research. I was trained as a statistician, which put me on the path to becoming a quantitative researcher, but quite quickly I realized that only with a more open-ended enquiry can you learn something really new.

Much brand research is done using qualitative research – most often focus group discussions. Whether it is for the development of a new brand, for developing and evaluating advertising or other elements of a brand's marketing mix, or for assessing the strengths and weaknesses of a brand at a point in time, the focus group discussion is the instrument of choice for getting a "quick fix" on the situation. The focus group does have its place; the much vaunted "group dynamics" can act as a stimulant for the emergence of ideas that might otherwise have remained dormant; specialized focus groups – those using psychodrama or role-playing, and groups of "expert" or creative consumers – have a very legitimate and distinctive purpose for certain types of enquiry. However, the main advantage of the focus group, and the main reason for its ubiquity, is a practical one; focus groups can be arranged and executed quickly, and the advent of the online group has made the process even faster; the research users can sit behind the one-way mirror or listen in to the group, and interact immediately and directly with the information that is emerging. Two or three evenings attending group discussions, followed by a wrap-up in the form of the group moderator's "top-line" report a couple of days later, really does give the impression of a job done, of the successful acquisition of marketplace information.

Group Discussions, however, have no place in researching the relational brand. It is not just that – the way a focus group project is carried out these days – there is rarely any time allowed for a proper content-analysis of the discussion by the group moderator, before reaching conclusions; and it is not just that most conclusions drawn from focus groups are phenomenological – based on a literal interpretation of what is said by the group participants; that there is rarely any attempt to generate second-degree constructs or hypotheses about the underlying consumer consensus. Simply, the focus group is the wrong instrument for understanding the relationship between a single consumer and a brand, because brand relationships are not a group phenomenon. This is not to say that we cannot eventually summarize and make general statements about a brand's relationship with different groups of consumers; but we have to understand its relationships with individual consumers *before* we add them together, which is the diametric opposite of what happens in a group discussion.

As explained in Chapter 2, according to the school of Relational Psychology relationships with a brand – relationships with any other object or person – contribute to the formation and development of the personality of the individual in that relationship. So, in researching consumer brand relationships we are in essence researching the personality of the informant, and that requires a particular type of research instrument, which is both clinical and intimate. At the very least it must be an individual interview, conducted one-on-one. Both the research instrument and the researcher must be as unobtrusive as possible, so as to avoid "contaminating" the content with their own relationships. This means using a non-directive form of questioning, which employs projective techniques in order to elicit responses, supplemented with very neutral follow-up probing. The ideal format is thus the individual depth interview (IDI) conducted by an experienced psychologist or moderator.

In contrast to the practicality of the focus group, an IDI research project will take longer to execute, requires a thorough content-analysis of the material (moderators must take notes during the interview), and then – in order to generate hypotheses about the brand relationships that have been identified – requires a second stage of analysis before conclusions are reached. Nor does it have the participative appeal of focus groups, as few research users will have either the time or the patience to sit through hours of on-on-one interviews. Another factor is, of course, cost; focus groups are by no means a low-cost option, but a typical four-group project can accumulate a "sample" of up to 50 people. To interview the same number of people individually will generally be significantly more costly. None of this should rule out the IDI as the instrument of choice for the first exploration of the brand relationships; but it does underline the necessity for an alternative, or supplementary, approach.

The so-called semi-structured interview – essentially an interviewer-administered questionnaire with open-ended questions – is a way of doing one-on-one interviews at a lower unit cost; it therefore offers the possibility of combining the benefits of qualitative research with the larger, more statistically reliable samples of quantitative research. A project involving just IDIs will inevitably require a follow-up quantitative study; the number of interviews – because of the cost and time factors – will be far too small to provide even a semblance of statistical representativeness. The semi-structured approach, on the other hand, can be carried out with respectably sized samples, and can, therefore, serve the purposes both of generating brand relationship constructs and of providing quantitative indications of their incidence among different segments of the brand's consumer franchise. Used with care, the semi-structured approach can preserve the richer, more divergent information typical of small-scale qualitative enquiries, but on a scale which permits the more convergent analytic framework of a quantitative study. So, we are not faced with the rigid choice of qualitative *or* quantitative research; we can have them both.

Two Methodological Approaches

1. Individual Depth Interviews with or without Quantitative Follow-On Study

Ideally, the project will start with Individual Depth Interviews, before proceeding to a separate quantitative survey. If the objective of the study is merely to map out the different types of consumer brand relationships that exist in a product category – or perhaps just for a single brand – then the project may just begin and end with the IDIs. If, at some later stage, quantification is required, then the IDIs will have provided the necessary hypotheses and parameters.

To some extent, the size of the qualitative project – the total number of interviews – will depend on whether the exploration of consumer brand relationships will remain just a qualitative one, or whether there will be a quantitative follow-up study. In the former case, the number of interviews should be larger, in order to make the stand-alone study more robust. In any case, the following parameters should guide construction of the sample.

- For each brand under examination, there should be samples of users and non-users or light/occasional users and heavy/loyal users.
- In some circumstances, you may also wish to include a sample of ex-users of the brand.
- If two or more brands are under examination, the cell sizes should be a minimum of five; they should be increased to at least ten for a study of just one brand. In other words, the total number of interviews will always be at least 20, and will increase by a minimum of ten for each additional brand.
- If the study is a stand-alone qualitative one, then consider increasing the total sample to a minimum of 30 or more interviews.[1]

The interview numbers quoted above of course refer to completed interviews, rather than the number of respondents recruited for the interviews. This may seem like an obvious distinction, but it reflects on the difference between IDIs and focus groups. In the latter, there is always someone talking; the more articulate, or voluble, members of the group can be relied on to pick up the slack and fill the silences left by their more taciturn colleagues. That doesn't happen in an IDI; and the particular nature of these interviews – it was not by chance that I described them above as "clinical and intimate" – may render some people more than usually speechless. Against this contingency, it is important to give your moderators "license to kill" the interview in its early stages, rather than pressing on into a possibly hostile silence. Over-recruit each cell by one or two in order to allow for this.

A protocol (known as the "BRAVE" protocol, the acronym of an early name that I gave to the methodology) has been developed for use in the interviews. Although the general format should be followed, it does not have to be adhered to in all its details. Different stimuli and different probes will work more or less effectively depending on the particular respondent, and the interviewers should adapt appropriately. It goes without saying that the interviewers must all be experienced in conducting IDIs.

The interview consists of two stages – a guided fantasy followed by a conventional exploration of brand images. The guided fantasy is conducted first because, after discussing everyday things like price and packaging, it can be difficult to get the respondent to "dream." In the guided fantasy, respondents are asked to imagine that they are dreaming and meet a person who personifies the brand; they are asked to describe the brand – what it looks like physically, its personality, how they feel about this person, and how they imagine its attitudes toward them. If possible, respondents are encouraged to hold a "conversation" with the brand (both sides of the conversation). The protocol for the first part of the interview can be found at the end of this appendix.

The interview should last between 25 and 45 minutes; the most important part is the guided fantasy, where only the most spontaneous and non-conditioned responses to the initial probes will represent real articulations of the brand's relationship with the consumer. For this reason, it is strongly recommended not to try and cover relationships with more than one brand with the same consumer. It is better to have a larger number of short interviews rather than a smaller number of long interviews, in which inevitably responses to the second brand will be rationalized and conditioned by the first set.

The analysis consists of two stages – first a conventional "descriptive" analysis of the interviews, and second an interpretative synthesis, which draws on the disciplines of semiotics (the symbolic meaning of words) and the analysis of archetypes in order to identify and describe the relationships. The secondary analysis, therefore, should be carried out by someone who is familiar with these disciplines and experienced in drawing out second-degree constructs from qualitative research.

2. Semi-Structured Interviews with No Follow-Up Quantitative Study

In this case, the research uses a questionnaire consisting of mainly open-end questions; it should also include (at the end of the interview) conventional pre-coded profile and relevant usage/behavioral information, against which the brand relationship classification can ultimately be cross-tabulated.

The open-end questions follow a similar sequence to the protocol for the IDIs, but are administered in a more standardized and fixed way. In fact, interviewers should be instructed not to paraphrase questions and to use only the specific probes written into the questionnaire. The key to the success of these interviews (as with IDIs) is the rapport between interviewer and respondent; the respondent has to know that it is OK to say "silly" things; that anything that comes into their mind to say is of interest to the interviewer. In this age of online research I know this will date me, but in my view this type of rapport can only be achieved in a face-to-face interview situation. The difference between this approach and the IDIs is in the standardization of the interview protocol, which enables the interview to be conducted by regular interviewers who are used to conducting face-to-face interviews, rather than by qualitative specialists or experienced moderators. The research can take place at central location research facilities, where interviewers with face-to-face experience are likely to be available. The other difference from IDIs is that the interviewers will generally not be involved in the analysis; although it can be useful to have a debriefing session with interviewers in order to get their impressions.

In order to reap the benefits of this hybrid "quali-quanti" approach, you need more than the questionnaire instrument; you also need an analytical approach that taps the disciplines of qualitative research and provides an output that can be summarized quantitatively.

The analysis consists of three phases – the first two qualitative, and the third quantitative.

- The first phase consists of reading the questionnaires and forming hypotheses about the nature of the relationships. This is essentially the same process of interpretive synthesis used for analyzing IDIs and should be carried out by people with the appropriate knowledge and experience. As a practical issue, the qualitative analysis team should consist of two or more researchers, at least one of whom has the necessary analytical skills and experience, and can instruct the other team members. Having discussed and agreed a preliminary set of relationship hypotheses, team members work independently to classify the brand relationships of a subset of the sample. They meet again to discuss and refine the classification scheme, and then work separately on new subsamples; this process is repeated until the classification scheme stabilizes. This iterative process requires both commitment and time from all the team members.
- At this point, the schema is formalized in a series of "pen portraits," ensuring that each analyst uses the same criteria for classifying brand relationships. The whole sample is then classified, according to the now agreed relationship schema, by at least two researchers working independently. My experience is that, at this stage, about 70 percent of the cases are classified similarly; classifying the remainder needs further discussion and resolution.
- Once a satisfactory level of convergence has been reached, the analysis switches to quantitative mode. Respondents' brand relationship classification is coded, so that conventional tabulation can be performed.

As with the IDI methodology, only one brand should be covered with each respondent; therefore, separate sample cells will be required for each brand in the study. For each brand under examination, there should be samples of users and non-users or light/occasional users and heavy/loyal users; in order to understand the brand's relationships with consumers who have either exited or are considering entering its franchise, you may also wish to take samples of ex-users of the brand and non-users who are interested in using the brand.

Quantitative Research Methodology

Generally, a custom quantitative study of brand relationships will be carried out in the context of a Usage and Attitude (U&A) Study. Alternatively, in these days of Big Data, the study may be conducted on a sample of respondents drawn from a panel, in order to match brand relationships with other data – for example, purchasing, media exposure, or internet activity – already on file about the same respondents. In either case, the aspect of methodology discussed here is confined to the module involving the measurement and analysis of brand relationships.

Data Collection

On the assumption that the relevant parameters – for measuring both brand perceptions (brand image) and brands' attitudes – have been identified, the data collection methodology is essentially the same as for any brand image study. You will therefore have to resolve all the usual methodological issues:

- the number of brands evaluated by each respondent
- minimum familiarity screening
- whether data collection will be "pseudo-monadic" (each brand evaluated in turn, one after the other) or comparative
- rating scales versus check-off associations.

Whatever the exact methodology chosen, it is highly recommended that the brand perceptions and brands' attitudes sections be completely separated, rather than having respondents switch backwards and forwards between the two. So, if you opt for the pseudo-monadic approach, complete the brand image questions for all brands before moving on to the brands' attitude questions. It is important to make the biggest distinction possible – within the limitations of what will probably be a self-administered internet interview – between the two types of evaluation that are being requested of the respondent. The question introduction should be completely different, with that for brands' attitudes making some reference to "using your imagination" in order to overcome resistance to the apparently "silly" idea of a brand thinking about "me" or doing things for "me." Ideally, if rating scales are being used, the wording of the scales should be different too; in contrast to the usual "Strongly Agree or Completely Agree," etc. of brand image scales, "Describes Completely" or "Definitely Applies," etc. are variations that might be used.

Apart from any necessary screening questions – including brand awareness and/or familiarity – the brand image and brands' attitudes segments should be completed before asking usage and other behavioral information.

Analysis

1. Data Cleaning

The data will probably be cleaned using a cleaning algorithm; data issues that should be eliminated in the cleaning, whether algorithmic or manual, include:

Incomplete data: A brand familiarity screening, whereby respondents are asked to evaluate only brands with which they have a minimal level of familiarity, will hopefully eliminate some of this problem. Fatigue, caused by being asked to evaluate too many brands on too many parameters, will lead to either brands or parameters being skipped. The latter is potentially a more serious problem as it may lead to the inability to classify relationships. Therefore criteria for the minimum number of parameters (separately for brand image and brands' attitudes) for inclusion in the data set should be established.

Response sets: Respondents' strategies for minimizing the use of mental resources on the interview are very common in internet surveys. They include "vertical" or "horizontal" checking – giving the identical responses for each brand or for each parameter. These response sets are clearly inimical to any analysis that is looking for meaningful patterns in the data, and they should be eliminated as far as possible.

2. Factor Analysis

Both sets of brand evaluations should be subject to factor analysis. I believe that factor analysis is an essential tool for identifying real outliers and for eliminating complete duplication between variables (by which I mean r values above say 0.7). However, I do not believe in using factor analysis slavishly in order to establish the metrics. Going into the analysis, there should be robust hypotheses, based on previous qualitative research, about the relevant brand image and brands' attitude factors that may constitute brand relationships; confirmation of these hypotheses – suitably modified – should be a guide to the choice of factor solutions. Do not, however, discard any strong factors (i.e. factors that appear in several different solutions) that were not part of the initial hypotheses; the next stage of analysis should attempt to integrate such factors into the relationship schema, as additional or alternative relationship components, which can then be evaluated.

Other issues that should be taken into account in the factor analyses are:

- Large general evaluative factors (these are usually the first principal component to emerge, and account for the highest proportion of total variance). Try to split this type of factor up by using a "Procrustes" analytical strategy; the simplest way is to do an analysis using only the variables that compose this factor, and specify a minimum number of factors (say two or three, depending on how many variables are in the analysis). Clearly, the resulting factors will be more highly inter-correlated than the others, but should be used if they preserve meaningful distinctions.
- From a theoretical point of view, I am agnostic about the type of rotation that should be used. In the UK, when I was training, I was taught to use an oblique rotation (e.g. Promax), which reduces the number of intermediate factor loadings

and maximizes the low and high loadings. However, on moving to the USA, I found the prevailing practice of using an orthogonal rotation (e.g. Varimax) quite satisfactory. In any case, I have rarely used the factor loadings in computing factor scores; if the variable makes sense, and contributes toward a better definition of the factor, then it should be included in the scoring with the same weight as the other variables. So, from a practical point of view, using an orthogonal rotation with the variables contributing equally to the factor score will probably result in a more clearly differentiated set of factors.

3. Determining the Brand Relationships Constructs

Each brand relationship is constructed by combining a specific brand image factor with a specific brands' attitude factor. In theory, the number of possible brand relationships is determined by the combinatorial possibilities of the two sets of component dimensions; so, if there are five brand image factors and five brands' attitude factors, you could construct up to 25 different brand relationships. In practice, of course, not all combinations have a relational logic to them, which will eliminate many of the theoretically possible combinations. For the rest, the relationship hypotheses, based on previous qualitative research, will be the primary guide for creating the quantitative relationship metrics, but you must be prepared to evaluate alternative and/or additional constructs at this stage. Inevitably, there will be some differences between your ingoing hypotheses and the possible combinations determined by your factors; so you will almost certainly have alternative candidates – either brand image or brands' attitude factors – for a given relationship; you will have to evaluate all of these to determine the optimal combination for each.

As explained in Chapter 2, true Brand Relationships have emergent properties, meaning that relationships should be *more than* just the sum – or average – of their two parts. What does that mean for evaluating alternative relationship constructs? As the whole purpose of measuring Brand Relationships (and of this book – see Chapter 1) is to gain a better understanding of and ability to influence consumers' purchasing behavior, the only relevant measures of *"more than"* are measures of different aspects of consumer behavior. This means that alternative relationship constructs should be evaluated in terms of their incremental ability to predict aspects of consumer behavior, over that of each of the separate components. In order to do that, a relationship metric must be calculated for each of the candidate relationships that are to be evaluated.

Any arbitrary arithmetical solution to combining the two components of a relationship, such as simple averaging, implies an additive assumption; which is contrary to the theory developed in Chapter 2, whereby relationships are composed of two essentially different components that interact in a non-additive manner. In Chapter 8, I discuss an empirical methodology that I used for calculating relationship metrics for the purpose of model building. This is, however, a very laborious method, which also requires "holding out" a different data set on which to test the constructs. For the purposes of evaluating alternative relationship constructs, a more practical methodology can be used, based on the concept of the two-dimensional relationship map. On a relationship map, a relationship score is plotted as the point defined by two coordinates; the x being (in the convention I have adopted) the brand image score, and the y being the brands' attitude score; the strength of the relationship is represented by the length of the vector joining that point to the origin of the map. A relationship score can thus be calculated, via a simple Pythagorean calculation, as the quadratic average of the two components' scores.[2]

Having obtained the brand relationship scores, the most direct method of evaluation of different relationship constructs is to calculate for each construct simple correlations between a series of behavioral variables and each of the following:

a)   the brand image score
b)   the brands' attitude score
c)   the brand relationship score.

When the brand relationship score correlates with a given behavioral variable, *more highly than either of its components do*, that is evidence of the emergent properties of the relationship construct, of synergy between the two components.

The following is a list of suggested behavioral variables; the specific objectives of the study – expanding the consumer franchise, increasing the loyalty of users, etc. – should be a guide as to which of these variables should be used and how they should be prioritized in determining the optimal brand relationship components.

- use/non-use of the brand
- time since last purchase
- purchase intent (non-users)
- purchase frequency (users)
- loyalty (users)
- price/value evaluation
- involvement with the brand on the internet and social media.

In evaluating a brand relationship construct, look for emergence between the two components across a range of behavioral variables. Where there are alternative constructs, all other things being equal, choose the one that shows the highest synergies across a broad range of behavioral variables or for the variables that are more important for your study's objectives.

Further Analyses

The types of analyses that are appropriate, once the structure of brands' relationships has been determined, can be broadly classified as consumer-based and brand based. The intention here is to provide just some suggestions for the type of analyses that are of specific relevance or appropriateness to consumer brand relationships, rather than to be totally comprehensive.

It is possible to use consumers' brand relationships as a basis for segmentation. For each brand, simply determine the strongest – i.e. highest scoring – brand relationship that each consumer has with the brand. If the sample includes non-users of the brand, you should set a minimum score (e.g. the bottom quartile of the distribution of scores) for the strongest brand relationship, below which consumers should be classified as "no brand relationship." The resulting brand relationship segments can be used in a variety of ways; for example:

- profiling by behavioral and other attitudinal data
- cross-tabbing of different brands' relationship segments, in order to reveal the role of brand relationships in determining competitive configurations between brands.

Brand-based analyses should certainly include brand relationship maps, of the type that I have used extensively throughout this book and particularly in Chapter 7. The maps can plot the relationships of multiple brands, in total and for subgroups; this provides the classic positioning overview of the brands in the market, in terms of their brand relationships. Additionally, maps can be used to plot the brand relationships of a single brand with different consumer segments – non-users, users, loyals, etc. This gives the clearest picture of the role of brand relationships at each point along the "funnel" of the brand's development.

For the types of analysis where you require a single "score" to represent the brand relationship, feel free to use the quadratic averaging method. But be aware that this involves an inevitable loss of information.

The "BRAVE" Protocol

Explain that this is a more creative, less literal type of interview; that we will be discussing brands of automobile in an unusual, playful way; that *anything* the respondent says is interesting. Ask respondents if they are willing "to play."

Explain the idea of bringing a brand to life as a person; that we are not necessarily talking about the person who sells the product, or the typical user, or the CEO of the company that markets it, but just the sort of person they might imagine who has all the characteristics they might associate with the brand. Use appropriate examples.

Personification

"I'd like you to close your eyes for a minute, and pretend you're dreaming. You know that in dreams you can see the craziest things – or they would be crazy if you weren't dreaming. In this dream you're having right now, I want you to imagine that a brand of automobile has turned into a person, and that this person has all the characteristics that you would associate with (brand). What would this person be like? Describe this person for me."

Personification Probes

- male/female
- age
- how dressed
- physical attributes (tall/short; thin/fat; attractive/plain)
- marital status
- family/household
- hobbies/interests/pastimes
- working? occupation? (blue/white collar)
- income (new/old money)
- lifestyle (neighborhood/house/car)
- personality/outlook on life.

"Imagine now that you have an opportunity to sit and chat with this (brand) person.

"On the basis of what the (brand) person is saying, and/or the way they talk/ hold themselves:

"What type of person is this? How does he/she come across to you?

"What is his/her outlook on life? What sort of views does he/she hold?"

Personality Probes

- outgoing/reserved
- old-fashioned/modern
- honest and straightforward/devious untruthful
- intelligent/stupid
- sophisticated/naive
- modest/braggart
- caring/cold
- generous/selfish
- risktaker/plays it safe
- formal/relaxed
- Is (brand) a happy person?
- Does he/she worry about anything?

Relationship Probes

- How do you feel about this person? What is your personal attitude toward this person (brand)?
- Do you like this person? How would you relate to this person? Do you want this person in your life?

- What would you want to say to him/her if you could be completely honest?
- Say you wanted to compliment him/her, what would you say?
- Say you wanted to be helpful to him/her, and give some advice, what would you say?
- What is (brand)'s attitude toward you?
- What does he/she think of you? How does he/she relate to you?
- What would he/she say to you if he/she were being completely honest?

Notes

1 For each new project, there is a definite learning curve in the process of analyzing the content, and identifying within it the consumer language that conveys the essence of different brand relationships. Without a sufficient number of interviews in total, there is a danger that you will not get high enough up that curve.

2 The relationship map calculation is as arbitrary as any other arithmetic formula, because, although the map is a very useful way of visualizing brand relationships, there is no a priori justification for calculating them as the resultant vector of orthogonal axes. It ensures that the construct will be monotonically increasing with respect to the two components, which, as I discuss in Chapter 8, is not necessarily the case. However, although the empirical method of scoring brand relationships that I described there is more purist – and leads to a better statistical fit in the model – the results are directionally the same as when quadratic averaging is used. In the spirit of methodological parsimony, it therefore appears to be "good enough" for the purposes of evaluating alternative constructs.

INDEX